Additional Praise for
Succession Planning for Financial Advisors

"I firmly believe *Succession Planning for Financial Advisors* is a fundamental addition to the library of any financial industry professional looking to implement a succession plan or to become a successor. Without a doubt, David Grau Sr. and the FP Transitions team understand the gauntlet of challenges. This resource provides practical tactics that take the pain out of planning a succession strategy to protect your clients and team members, and build a practice that outlives you for generations to come."

—Andrea Schlapia, founder/CEO, Ironstone, Inc.

"A must read for advisors who are serious in planning for their clients and their companies future. I use the motto 'think things through and follow through'. This step-by-step guide will help advisors get their planning completed and enjoy life more!"

—Maureen McAnarney, co-president,
VSR Financial Services

"FP Transitions' book gives financial advisors a vital road map for turning a professional practice into an enduring business, which will serve their own financial security while it preserves the well-being of their clients."

—James "Chip" Mahan, CEO, Live Oak Bank

"I have followed David's and FP Transitions' articles for years. His statistical research and, more importantly, his first-hand experience provide an uncanny insight as to how a financial service firm typically evolves and what it takes to create a market for that firm. He and the FP Transitions' team unmask the shortcomings of the traditional compensation arrangements promoted by insurance companies and brokerage houses and provide producers a better way to compensate themselves and ultimately monetize their many years of hard work. This book is a must-read for all financial service professionals."

—Donald L. Reichert, MSFS, CLU, ChFC, AEP®, CAP;
president, Capital Design Associates

"You must read this book as one of the first steps in creating your succession plan and embarking on such a significant venture. We all can acknowledge how so many advisors are unprepared in this vital area. Arm yourself with this valuable information gleaned from years of experience in just this arena. David and FP Transitions have examined so many elements to the challenge making it far more possible to execute a viable transition for your firm. Why stumble along yourself with no plan in mind when a professional has created a game plan for you? Buy this book and get started!"

—Diane MacPhee, CFP® PCC, nationally recognized
business coach for Financial Advisors,
www.dmacconsulting.org

"Being a financial planner/advisor requires a multitude of skills that are not necessarily innate or part of our professional training. Through the evolution from sales person to fiduciary the demand for a consistent, perpetuating organization has grown and will continue to grow in the future. David and FP Transitions' book *Succession Planning: Building an Enduring Business* is not simply about reaping the benefits from past labors (although that is part of it), but about fulfilling the promise we have made to our clients that we will be there when they need us. Truly keeping our clients interest's first."

—Martin Kurtz, CFP, president, CEO, The Planning Center, Inc.;
past president, Financial Planning Association (2011)

Succession Planning for Financial Advisors

Succession Planning for Financial Advisors

Building an Enduring Business

DAVID GRAU SR., JD
AND THE △ FP TRANSITIONS® TEAM

WILEY

Cover Design: Wiley
Cover Image: © iStock.com/PPAMPicture

Published by John Wiley & Sons, Inc., Hoboken, New Jersey.
Published simultaneously in Canada.

For general information on our other products and services or for technical support, please
contact our Customer Care Department within the United States at (800) 762-2974, outside
the United States at (317) 572-3993, or fax (317) 572-4002.

Wiley publishes in a variety of print and electronic formats and by print-on-demand. Some
material included with standard print versions of this book may not be included in e-books or
in print-on-demand. If this book refers to media such as a CD or DVD that is not included in
the version you purchased, you may download this material at http://booksupport.wiley.com.
For more information about Wiley products, visit www.wiley.com.

Library of Congress Cataloging-in-Publication Data:

Grau, David, Sr.
  Succession planning for financial advisors : building an enduring business / David Grau, Sr.
    pages cm
  Includes index.
  ISBN 978-1-118-86647-4 (cloth); ISBN 978-1-118-86641-2 (ePDF);
ISBN 978-1-118-86642-9 (ePub)
  1. Financial planners. 2. Executive succession. 3. Financial services industry—
Management. I. Title.
  HG179.5.G727 2014
  658.1′6—dc23

                                                                            2014012693

Printed in the United States of America.
10 9 8 7 6 5 4 3 2 1

Contents

Preface

This book is going to challenge you and everything you think you know about succession planning. As an independent advisor, you own what you do, you are unique, and you are responsible for building something that will outlive you—something that is tied to the lifetimes of the clients you serve. We're going to show you how to do just that.

Along the way, we are going to point out the challenges that lie in your path to building a multigenerational business. But we're also going to help you build the bridges to get there. As a guide, you need to know something more about the sources of knowledge and data that support the findings and conclusions and recommendations in the pages that follow.

FP Transitions is now 16 years old. I work there, and along with my partner Brad Bueermann, we are the first-generation owners and caretakers of our business. During our time together and aided by a fantastic cast and crew, here is what we have done with you and for you: (1) More than 5,000 valuations of independent financial services and advisory practices have been completed (at the current and increasing rate of about 120 valuations per month), all with five-year histories of revenue and growth; (2) more than 1,000 personalized benchmarking studies have been completed and delivered using the data from the valuation intake process (not survey data); (3) more than 1,200 closed transactions (sales or mergers to third parties) have been completed; (4) more than 1,750 continuity plans have been implemented and supported annually with valuations and updated agreements and funding mechanisms; (5) more than 300 internal ownership tracks have been set up and maintained for businesses and firms in this industry; (6) more than 400 new, next-generation advisors have been made owners through these internal ownership tracks; and (7) more than 1,000 speaking engagements and workshops have been completed to date. In addition, we have been hired to set up entities or to consult on the adjustments or recapitalization of more than 250 entity structures per year to make them work in this industry. There are 20,000 current registered clients who use FP Transitions' site and information sources at any given time, 1,500 of whom now pay monthly subscription fees (a service first offered just five years ago), with another 500 signing up or renewing each year.

In our "shipbuilding program" (more on that later), we spend thousands upon thousands of hours every year going over the details of your practices and your business dreams and goals.

That's a lot of information and data, and our Research and Analytics team is charged with organizing it so that our collective experiences and knowledge can be channeled through this book and subsequently focused on helping you achieve your succession planning goals. To that end, we spend our days working with independent advisors to help you build valuable and enduring business models. We're learning with you, in a young and dynamic industry. Sharing these experiences as we explore the path forward is the purpose of this book.

Acknowledgments

First, let me thank the only girlfriend I've ever had, my wife of 35 years, Penny. She has supported every dream I've ever had whether they made sense or not. Every day she shares with me her special gifts—a smile and a great attitude, and endless patience. Being married to an entrepreneur means a lot of time alone, not just the time to write this book, but the preceding decades it took to amass the knowledge and experience and education. As I work through yet another million miles of travel across the country on behalf of FP Transitions, I am thankful that she has been rescued by our four small dogs that don't believe in alone time.

One of the points we make in this book is that businesses are not built alone. My business partner, Brad Bueermann, is nothing short of my coauthor. When he joined FP Transitions, it was to serve as our second stage rocket booster. We had gotten off the ground, as you'll read, but we likely would never have achieved orbit but for his wisdom and foresight—Brad showed me firsthand that it often takes a different set of skills to transition from a job or a practice into a business of enduring value. There is not one page of this book that he has not touched or improved. He was also the only person courageous enough to suggest that the book's first draft would make a wonderful contribution to Oregon's renowned recycling efforts.

Brad lives a simple, but sophisticated business life based on two fundamental tenets: (1) constantly explore new territory, and (2) have fun doing it. It has been my honor over the past decade to have known him and worked alongside him.

The authors of this book also include the FP Transitions team. You'll notice that the common voice in this book is not "I," but "we," and that reflects the people who make up our own enduring business. We have learned, firsthand, that working as a team allows us to learn more and to learn faster; we avoid mistakes by questioning and challenging each other. We fight, we scrap, and we work for every last detail and ounce of success, and when we find it, we share it and then immediately look to the horizon for what's next, and what's possible. Sometimes we bump our heads, and sometimes we just collectively start over, but *ordinary* and *run-of-the-mill* are bad words to us. We like to push the boundaries and challenge people and each other, and that is what makes our work fun. Like the readers of this book, we're building a business to make a difference.

Finally, thanks must go to all of the independent advisors out there who let us practice on them—there has been a steep learning curve, to be sure. People often credit us with being pioneers in this industry, and, while Brad and I and our team smile and offer humble thanks, deep down we're thinking, "If they only knew. . . ."

Introduction

Being an independent financial professional necessarily implies a commitment to a profession that surpasses a single career; the element of planning, or at least focusing on the future, implies that you're starting something that will not and should not end with your own career.

Ninety-five percent of independent financial services professionals are one-owner practices. To the positive, these practices are among the most valuable professional service models in the United States. But almost all are assembling their practices using the wrong tools—tools borrowed from historically successful, but vastly different models, including wirehouses, broker-dealers, and even offices of supervisory jurisdiction (OSJs) and branch managers. Revenue-sharing, commission-splitting and other eat-what-you-kill compensation methods dominate the independent sector and virtually ensure that today's independent practices, if left unchanged, will not survive the end of their founder's career. Independent business models need different building and assembly tools, because of one major difference—independent advisors own the value they're building, not their broker-dealers or the custodian they associate with—and that ownership carries with it significant rewards, and opportunities, and obligations. It's no longer about having a job, yet that's exactly how most independent owners approach their practices. Why create a succession plan for a practice designed all along to be just one-generational?

Of course, much of this problem could be solved, or at least substantially mitigated, if one were to assume that independent practice owners would eventually sell or otherwise intentionally transfer their client relationships to another, younger advisor or to a larger firm upon retirement. But the data on this point are clear as well. Entrepreneurs rarely sell. Financial services practice owners strongly prefer to hold on to their predictable revenue-producing practices as long as possible, even as they decline and begin to wind down on their own. Advisors unnecessarily opt for the ongoing cash flow associated with their work in exchange for the equity value and ability—perhaps *duty* is the better word—of professionally transferring the relationships and assets to a handpicked successor who could perpetuate the services for another generation.

There is a solution, and all of the tools and knowledge to implement it already exist. Simply stated, the solution requires the coordination of a proper ownership-level compensation system and the ability to gradually monetize the equity value of every business in this industry as part of a long-term, multiple-generational growth strategy, part of a process we call *equity management*. The concept of equity management is as new and young as the independent side of this industry, and it is just as powerful. To build a sustainable business, you have to manage cash flow and equity professionally, and helping you take the first important steps to mastering that concept is one of the most important goals of this book.

This book and the instruction it provides are intended for use by the following four groups:

1. Practices that want to take the next step and grow into a business
2. Owners who are looking to create long-term cash flow or a legacy
3. Intrepid employees and junior partners (and sons and daughters) who want to initiate a discussion about succession planning and an ownership opportunity
4. Independent broker-dealers, custodians, and insurance companies that need to understand how to create enduring businesses and why that is every bit as important as generating production and recruiting more producers

That said, the lessons provided in this book are applicable to a much wider audience, including wirehouse or captive advisors who are contemplating the move to independence, insurance agents who understand the value of predictable revenue and the equity it generates, as well as the attorneys, accountants, coaches, and recruiters for all of the aforementioned. Finally, as a former securities regulator, I suggest that those who write and enforce the myriad rules and regulations for this industry (state and federal regulators, and the compliance officers at the independent broker-dealers, custodians, and insurance companies) can gain a much better understanding of the differences between captive and independent advisors, enabling them to gradually adjust the regulatory scheme to support the building of strong and enduring businesses that can, in turn, support a client's needs well beyond the advisor's career.

With the aim clear and steady, let's focus on the goal: The independent financial services industry should be the leader, the best of all professional service models when it comes to planning for the future. As an industry, we have to work together to reset the table and get this process started. With this book, we'll give you the tools to succeed.

CHAPTER 1

The Succession Conundrum

PRACTICES BUILT TO DIE

As an industry, we have a problem to solve: 99 percent of today's independent financial services and advisory practices will not survive their founder's retirement or the end of the founder's individual career. When the advisor leaves, for whatever reason, it's over. And that has to change.

In many professions and in most businesses, this is not a problem. You don't need a multigenerational dentist or dental firm, for instance. Who cares if your neighborhood hamburger stand has a succession plan? But in this industry, it is different. Wealth doesn't have a lifetime. Even so, clients have a clear expectation of advice tailored to the length of their lives, not to the length of their advisor's career. Clients do have a choice—they can choose between a career-length practice (or possibly even shorter upon the death or disability of a single owner) and the multigenerational wirehouse (think Bank of America/Merrill Lynch, Wells Fargo, UBS). The independent industry seized the momentum from the wirehouses (at least in terms of popularity) over the course of the recession, but may well cede it back in years to come unless this problem is resolved.

So, specifically, who are we talking about—to whom does this "99 percent" statement apply? The list certainly includes independent registered representatives and advisors, whether under an independent broker-dealer or custodian or insurance company. The list includes stand-alone Registered Investment Advisers (RIAs), as well as the investment advisor representatives (IARs) who work under someone else's RIA and own their own practices or books (in the pages that follow, we collectively refer to all these professionals as "advisors"). The list also includes investment professionals who are fee-only, fee-based, or commission-based. The list includes the smallest of the lot with annual production or gross revenues of $100,000 to $150,000 a year, as well as the largest we've worked with to date at around $20 million in annual production or gross revenues, and everything and everyone in between. The list includes new start-ups, as well as older, established businesses and firms whose tenures match their founders' many years in the industry. The list also includes most accountants, tax professionals, and estate planners who are licensed or authorized to provide investment advisory or other financial services. All are equally unprepared. All their practices are built to die or fade away after one generation of ownership.

While encompassed in the preceding list, it merits pointing out that all the investment professionals who call themselves or otherwise function as silos for practical purposes are the people we're talking about as well (*silo* is the term many advisors use when referring to multiple owners/producers under one roof, with each servicing and owning one's own group of clients). More surprisingly, most ensembles are also included in that 99 percent group (the term *ensemble* refers to a formal team arrangement); rarely have we come across a group of advisors who call themselves an ensemble that has the ability and the enterprise strength as a business to turn the corner into the second generation of ownership—and those who do are starting the process too late with no clue as to how long it takes to implement an internal ownership transition.

To be clear, we're not saying for one minute that independent advisors can't make a very good living (they can and are doing so for the most part); they're just falling short of building an enduring business. Today's independent advisors are not failing in their work of providing professional and relevant and much-needed financial services and advice to their clients; they are failing to sustain a business beyond their own careers, leaving their clients to do that portion of the planning on their own, and advisors (and their broker-dealers, custodians, and insurance companies) are leaving an incredible amount of money on the table as a result for no good reason.

As an industry, we've arrived at this point together and certainly not as a result of making a lot of mistakes. One of the reasons the independent sector has grown as fast as it has is through competition. Entrepreneurs are great competitors! In terms of number of advisors and annual revenue growth rates, the independent side of this industry just plain works. What's missing is the endurance factor—businesses that can survive the founder's retirement, death, or disability—and that will come from collaboration as much as competition. The idea of collaboration is woven throughout a formal succession plan.

WHAT EXACTLY IS A SUCCESSION PLAN?

In this industry, and in this book, a succession plan is best defined as a professional, written plan designed to build on top of an existing practice or business and to seamlessly and gradually transition ownership and leadership internally to the next generation of advisors. The business itself continues on, not just the life of many or some of its individual assets. To accomplish these goals, the business has to get stronger, and it has to grow, and that is why conquering this problem is such a tremendous opportunity for this young and evolving industry and everyone associated with it.

In the process of helping you figure out how best to consider and construct your succession plan, we would be remiss not to also cover the related concepts of exit planning and replacement planning, which provide some much-needed relief and realization of value to the late starters or the smaller practice owners who, for one reason or another, will not be building an enduring business. In fact, exit planning is where FP Transitions started back in 1999, and for many years we, like many of you, thought of selling your practice at the end of your career as the solution or at least as something almost as good as a formal succession plan. Based on the number of articles we read every month in the industry publications, it is clear that succession planning and selling are often thought of as one and the same; but they are not.

So we need to set the record straight and come clean on this point as well. Selling your practice to a larger, stronger, multigenerational business can be a good strategy, and for many of today's older and single-owner advisors, it is quite simply the best and fastest solution when the time comes. But for the rest of this industry, the thought of selling when you're done working in your practice is not a plan—it is a recipe for procrastination. One of the things we've learned from you over the past 16 years is that entrepreneurs rarely sell. The idea of one day walking away and no longer being regulated or depended on by so many clients through the tough economic stretches is exhilarating, and tempting, especially on those bad days in the office. That's understandable.

Too often, however, the concept of planning gets confused with merely an idea or some evolving thoughts over the years about what you could do when that time comes. In truth, absent a serious health condition or a new passion in your life, "that time" never comes. The cash flow is too tempting and too rewarding to walk away from, the workweeks grow shorter, retirement is postponed, and then, one day, there's nothing of substantial value left to sell or plan with. We see it all the time—so often, in fact, we have a name for it: attrition. The act of thinking about selling your practice one day in the future most often results in your taking no action steps to strengthen or grow your practice in the meantime, and it continually ends with one result: The practice dies on its own as you get older and spend less time, energy, and money running it. Attrition is the number one exit strategy in the independent industry today, by a wide margin, and is a leading contributor to the 99 percent death rate of independent practices after the first generation of ownership.

Together, we can do better. As we consider how to shift gears from a one-generational practice to an enduring and valuable business, you need to think about the first step in the process—just one single step in the right direction. It's easy and it is powerful and it starts with a single word: *planning*. That might seem obvious, but too many advisors start with other words like *selling* or *dying* or *slowing down* or *losing control*. Those are powerful words, too, but they tend to prompt inaction and fear. Succession planning is about building and strengthening your practice or business; it is about retaining control over an enterprise, and, in time, it really is about working smarter and not harder, and it is about being financially rewarded for a career well spent for the rest of your life.

Planning is about taking stock of your situation. It is about surrounding yourself with the right people who can help you make smart decisions; it is about gathering facts and information and having a thorough understanding of your best choices and the costs and benefits of implementing each one. (Note that executing a buy-sell agreement is not a succession plan or a substitute for planning—more on that later.) As your chosen and purposeful plan unfolds, be it a succession plan, an exit plan, or a replacement plan, you will be creating a pathway into the future that you control, a pathway that you can share and explain to your family and your staff and your clients. Planning is the critical first step, and it is so much more than just an idea.

WHY YOU NEED TO CREATE A SUCCESSION PLAN NOW

For many independent advisors, succession planning is becoming the cornerstone to a strategic growth strategy designed to perpetuate their business and their income streams beyond their own lifetimes, and this makes succession planning one of the most important practice management tools, if not *the* most important one, in this industry today. But for many advisors who have not begun the process or remain unsure of embarking on this course there are three simple reasons why you need a succession plan and you need to start on it now:

1. It is the best way to realize the value of a lifetime of work.
2. It is the best way to recruit next-generation talent to grow your business.
3. It is the best way to preserve and protect what you've built.

Succession planning is not an end-game strategy for your business; it is not about shutting things down and calling it a day. If anything, succession planning is about building a bigger, stronger business that can one day work for you. With a good plan, the right people, and enough time, every business can survive its founder's retirement and many can even prosper. That might sound scary if you've built an egocentric practice, but from your clients' perspective, it makes total sense.

Realizing the Value of a Lifetime of Work

For most independent financial services professionals and advisors, their practices are the single most valuable asset they own, always a six-figure proposition, and many times a seven-figure number or more at its peak. Regardless, it will have a major impact on your own retirement plans even if you hope to work forever. To be certain, it is the one asset you exert almost total control over.

There is little push-back from advisors we talk to regarding the role their business plays in their lives—it is an important asset. But some advisors consider the value of their practices to lie primarily in cash flow, the money they take home every month and year after year in exchange for the work that they do. If the practice is small enough and has no infrastructure around it, this might be true; but for most independent advisors, that approach is too limited. Independent financial services professionals enjoy a distinct and important advantage over captive advisors—they have two kinds of value to work with to reward themselves, to build with, and to use to attract and retain next-generation talent: cash flow + equity.

To build an enduring and transferable business, advisors must learn how to utilize both types of value simultaneously, and that is exactly what a well-constructed succession plan will do. Building a business around both cash flow and equity value is what separates a one-generational job or practice from a more valuable and enduring business. A properly designed succession plan can perpetuate income (cash flow) while gradually realizing equity value (at long-term capital gains rates) as next-generation advisors invest and buy into your business. Cash flow is what advisors work for; equity is what owners invest in.

Most advisors have heard the rules of thumb that a practice is worth about two times trailing 12 months recurring revenue. While that's in the ballpark, that is the number when selling to a larger, stronger buyer, quite likely a business. Building your own business and selling your stock or ownership interest very gradually to a team of next-generation advisors as the value continually grows is a far more lucrative proposition—if you give it the time it deserves by planning early enough. An internal ownership transition can provide a multiple of five to seven times the starting point (based on trailing 12 months revenue), not including wages and benefits over the course of the plan, which are significant in their own right.

You owe it to yourself and your family to realize the highest value from what you have built at the best possible tax rates. A carefully constructed succession plan will do just that.

Recruiting Next-Generation Talent to Grow Your Business

You have many choices to make as an independent owner. One is whether to focus on growing just your cash flow (think office of supervisory jurisdiction [OSJ], broker-dealer, or wirehouse model); another is growing your equity value prior to exiting. A succession plan will help you grow both cash flow and equity.

Succession plans depend on next-generation talent. If you're growing a business, odds are you won't be working on a replacement plan for yourself by finding "another you," but rather a plan that relies on a team of successors— two, three, maybe four people, all at least 10 to 15 years younger than you are, to work together, to do what each does best, to cumulatively buy out your position over 10 years or more in many cases. You're going to need a bigger boat and more people. This concept also means that you have another important choice to make when hiring, training, and compensating your staff members, including those already on board: Will you help them become collaborators or competitors?

When younger advisors are recruited into an individual practice that has no future beyond the career or life of its founder and that founder is in the last 10 years of his or her career, the natural tendency is for the new recruits to build their own practices, or books—there is no better choice. If there is no enduring business to invest in, the next generation of advisors will start to build their own practices. This is what most incoming advisors are faced with today, but a business with a succession plan can offer something very different, something much better—a career, and an ownership opportunity that comes with a paycheck and a mentor. That's an enticing package for someone with a career to invest.

The difference between owning a job as an independent financial services professional and having a job on the captive side of the industry can be hard to distinguish sometimes. The difference is equity, but if the only access to equity value is to start your own business from scratch, the independent side will attract only entrepreneurs and way too few of the very necessary support and role players to give a practice the ability to become a real and enduring business. A succession plan isn't about your retirement as the founder; it is about empowering you so you can share what you've spent a career learning with next-generation advisors who work for you, learn from you, and then invest in what you've built—collaborative partners instead of competitive former staff members.

Preserving and Protecting What You've Built

Contrary to popular lore, entrepreneurs are not immortal or invincible. One day, one way or another, you will be leaving your practice behind by choice or by fate; plan for both possibilities.

One of the biggest threats to a one-owner advisory practice (the most common ownership structure among independent financial services professionals) is not the lack of a succession or retirement plan or exit strategy for the founding owner, but the lack of a plan to protect the clients and the owner's value in the event of the owner's sudden death or disability. Continuity planning seeks to address the question of who will serve as advisor to the clients if their primary advisor is incapacitated; it is an important first step to most comprehensive succession plans.

The challenges and solutions in developing a continuity plan can be very different from those used to create or implement a succession or retirement plan. For some professionals, the first and only solution is to purchase a life insurance policy—a solution that almost completely ignores the welfare of the clients. But in fairness, what choices does a one-owner practice have? How can you protect a one-owner practice against a six-month absence due to a temporary disability resulting from something unforeseen like a car accident or a heart attack or cancer? Succession planning provides the answer; remember the definition of a succession plan is that it incorporates a gradual transition of ownership and leadership to the next generation of advisors, preferably a team of advisors. It doesn't matter that your younger business partner owns only 10 percent or 20 percent of the business—it matters that he or she is an owner and a collaborative partner. An internal ownership plan, once implemented, is the single best continuity plan available.

Think about it: Who best to protect the value and the relationships you've spent a lifetime building than another owner who has invested in the business and who needs to protect this shared value until you return? For most 30-year-olds, that minority ownership position is, or will be, the largest, most valuable asset they own. If they're part of your succession team, all the better. A succession plan provides answers on many levels.

YOUR CLIENTS ARE WATCHING YOU!

Every day, we hear from our 50-, 60-, and 70-year-old advisory clients that they are being repeatedly asked the question: "What happens to me if something happens to you?" In a *Time* magazine article (July 18, 2013), writer Dan Kadlec addressed these issues, warning clients of independent advisors to start asking questions and exploring their options. Here is his excellent advice, in part:

> *If you have a financial adviser, odds are this person is contemplating his or her own retirement, as well as yours. If you have an older financial adviser, you need to:*
>
> - *Understand the coming transition. Ask now about your adviser's retirement date and how he or she intends to handle your account. Do you want to stay with the firm? Do you want to try someplace new? Do you want your adviser to handpick a successor? How quickly will someone new get up to speed?*
> - *Look for an upgrade. You may be happy with your adviser but there's always room for improvement. This is your chance to re-set expectations and clarify how your needs are changing. Make this clear and you'll get something out of the transition besides a headache.*
> - *Ask questions. You want to know all your options if you get notified about a transition. That means you have to take charge—and you should always feel free to change the relationship if the balance of fees for service no longer feels right.*

Your clients deserve better answers than hearing that you have a good idea on how to handle such events when they arise or that you'll make a plan when you're older and have more time. As the information increases on this subject matter, scrutiny will increase, too. You can hope that you'll retire before it gets too bad, or that you can talk your way through it—but is that enough? Is that a satisfactory set of actions by an independent owner in the financial services industry? In truth, your clients and their children will choose their own answers to these questions, maybe with the help of a competitor across town who owns an enduring business model.

A succession plan will show that you care about their long-term financial future. Your succession plan ensures that your talents and the knowledge and culture that you have built into your practice are being transferred to the next generation and can be relied upon by your clients into the future. To do that, you're going to need to expand the ownership base to include one or two or three next-generation advisors, and you're going to need to be their mentor for a long time to come, hiring and retaining only the best so that your clients will enjoy a seamless and professional transition. Along the way, your successors will learn what your clients want for their own children and grandchildren, and that critical knowledge and expertise will make the transition within your business from one generation of ownership to the next.

WHY THIS INDUSTRY STRUGGLES WITH THIS CONCEPT

So if creating a succession plan carries so many advantages to owners, their clients, and their employees, why do we not have an industry-wide solution? Why are there so few succession plans and so many practices that will die with this generation of owners?

In our experience there are many reasons, but we see four primary issues that help explain why this industry and the independent reps and advisors who populate it are struggling when it comes to building enduring business models capable of multigenerational ownership.

First, the tools and strategies that are being used to assemble today's independent practices have been borrowed from the wirehouse industry and were never intended for use by independent advisors. These tools, which commonly include some form of a compensation system based solely on production or revenue sharing—what we term an eat-what-you-kill approach—is a central problem preventing owners and their employees from viewing their business as a single enterprise rather than a collection of individual client books.

The original goal of generating greater and greater production is being solved primarily through competition (i.e., many individual books in a produce-or-starve format) rather than collaboration (a group of owners working in concert in a single business), because that is the easier and faster approach in the short run. You can learn to produce something in fairly short order; building a business takes time and skill. The wirehouse model and even most of the insurance company models have thrived on this approach, and it works well because the enduring business still exists—it is the wirehouse or insurance company itself. In the independent space, advisors are tasked with building their own enduring businesses, but the lack of collaborative and prospective equity partners is stopping the process cold. In many ways, advisors' struggle to create successors has more to do with building than with planning.

Second, a portion of the blame must also be directed at the way the rules governing this industry were written and how they are interpreted and administered. Financial Industry Regulatory Authority (FINRA) rules and regulations make it difficult for many of today's advisors to operate effectively as their own enterprises; advisors from both sides of the industry (captive and independent) are treated the same even though they are obviously very different—independent advisors own what they do. First-generation independent owners have equity in addition to cash flow, and they can use that equity to attract and provide a long-term, tax-efficient reward to those who invest in their small businesses—what you'll come to learn is a staple in every succession plan.

Third, today's independent practice owners come from a sales culture, which is now being passed on to the next generation. The roots of this industry are firmly tied to production and sales. The result of this sales culture has often been to build practices that simply focus on increasing production as efficiently and quickly as possible and not on building enterprise strength or long-term value. Many advisors were encouraged along these lines by their broker-dealers or custodians and still are by many of today's coaches. Have you ever heard of recognition awards given for highest firm value or strongest service model? Production, as measured in gross revenue or assets under management, remains the primary yardstick of success for advisors. But this is changing as independent practice owners realize that their own goals and those of their practice might be better served by concentrating on building enterprise strength and value resulting in enduring businesses that attract and retain the best of next-generation talent, rather than simply constructing a so-called revenue mill that will stop when they do.

Fourth, independent broker-dealers, custodians, and insurance companies share some of the blame as well and some of the responsibility for helping to fix things. There are two predominant views in the independent space when it comes to succession planning: (1) that it is the advisor's problem and sole responsibility, and/or (2) that selling is the best and most common exit strategy. Accordingly, broker-dealers and custodians consistently adopt a defensive strategy to keep the assets within the network by putting up a matching site so the advisor can easily sell to another rep or advisor within the same network. Here, too, the thinking is beginning to change as independent broker-dealers realize that they need to help their advisors create enduring businesses in order for the assets to stay within their networks. They also are realizing that it is not in anyone's best interest to let practices that they have recruited and nurtured simply wither and die when they can be saved and grown for decades to come by creating a succession plan.

A multilevel problem needs a multilevel solution. Said more directly, a broader solution set for the independent advisory industry must involve independent broker-dealers and custodians, and clearing companies, and insurance companies, and industry organizations such as the Financial Planning Association (FPA), National Association of Personal Financial Advisors (NAPFA), Life Insurance Marketing and Research Association (LIMRA), and Investment Management Consultants Association (IMCA), as well as the independent advisors, reps, and insurance agents whose practices are at risk of declining—when they should be growing and multiplying and building upon each generation. Paying more lip service to the idea of a succession plan, and creating more match-making sites, just won't cut it anymore. But the first step belongs to the advisors, who simply are not in a position to wait for the industry to catch up and adjust and support their real needs. Fortunately, entrepreneurs are perfectly suited to taking on a challenge that provides so many benefits.

THE EVOLUTION OF THE SOLUTION

This is a relatively new industry, at least in terms of having independent practices with substantial equity value. Even RIAs, which by definition are independent, have not, except in the case of the largest businesses, had any realizable value in the past.

I remember receiving a call when I was a new lawyer around 1994 from one of my RIA clients. He said to me, "I think I'm done. It's time to do something else. I have $50 million in assets under management, 45 great clients. Do you suppose anyone would want them?" In the end, he did find someone who wanted them. The deal structure they agreed to was a zero down, 10-year earn-out arrangement at a multiple of 1.25 times trailing 12 months revenue. It was a fee-only practice.

The normal approach to retirement in this industry 20+ years ago was to send a note to the clients saying "It has been a pleasure . . ." and attaching a list of advisors in the area that they could contact for help and advice. So, given that this is the first generation of advisors with almost universal value, that is to say that almost all practices can be sold today in an organized and competitive marketplace, it is not surprising that advisors are struggling with a succession solution. After all, there is no model to follow, no set pattern or template from which to navigate, no history as to how to do it. People have called us pioneers for creating the open marketplace and launching concepts that include an accurate and affordable valuation system and equity management; but in many ways you're all pioneers, too, and we're going to have to blaze this next trail together.

In the absence of an established succession model, the idea of succession in this industry has been almost revolutionary. Very slowly, advisors have been coming to grips with the notion that their practices have value, in many cases a great deal of value, and that they need to have at least a modicum of a plan to realize that value. Advisors are also realizing that cash flow and equity are two different things. The recent recession seems to have provided further strength and momentum to these trends. In addition, more and more advisors are embracing the responsibility that they have to their clients to provide some form of continuity of services from one generation to the next. But many of those revelations are of relatively recent origin. It was very different 15 to 20 years ago.

The first formal model of succession to be adopted in this industry was to systematically sell the practice to the best-qualified candidate, a concept that FP Transitions helped pioneer. Founded in 1999, FP Transitions began around the nascent need for a systematic way to find a buyer for a practice and handling the myriad details to successfully sell the practice, realize value, and transition the trusting client relationships en masse. Since its founding, FP Transitions has sold over a thousand financial services and advisory practices of all sizes and under a variety of circumstances and for a broad range of values. Fast-forward, and the system for buying and selling practices and transitioning client relationships is well established—it works. So succession is mostly solved, right? Not quite, because as it turns out, selling is *not* succession planning; but selling, as a strategy, was the necessary first step to establishing and proving the concept of value in this industry, and that was an incredibly important accomplishment.

On that point, understand that the average value of a CPA's practice is about 1.0 times trailing 12 months revenue. Doctors, dentists, lawyers, architects, and many other professional service models sell for slightly less than a 1.0 times multiple, depending on the terms of the deal. Most of those professionals have had access to Small Business Administration (SBA) bank financing and a myriad of business brokers to help them buy and sell their practices and businesses. Independent financial professionals have a much younger organized marketplace, have had no formal bank financing support until recently, and still have a value proposition of two to three times that of any of the more learned professions. And we're just getting started!

The average buyer-to-seller ratio for a practice listed for sale through FP Transitions is 50 to 1; that means that 50 interested buyers step forward in the first 10 days a practice is listed for sale and disclose pertinent information about themselves, including name, contact information, recent valuation results, affiliations and credentials, and qualifications and experience, to a confidential and unnamed seller. Nine out of 10 serious and well-informed sellers find a best match and acceptable price and terms and close the transaction in under eight weeks. In other words, the listing and selling system developed by FP Transitions is extremely efficient.

Yet, over the past 16 years of running the largest national platform for buying and selling practices, a curious fact has emerged: Based on our experience and review of a mountain of data (i.e., 5,000-plus valuations, 1,750 continuity plans, etc.), it turns out that only about 8 percent of independent practice owners will ever sell their practice or business. How do we know for sure? We've been tracking the data from the practices that we have valued and worked with. All the pundits writing articles in the industry press, as well as the executives of broker-dealers and custodians who developed strategies to handle the flood of potential sales of their aging advisors missed a critical point: Entrepreneurs—independent practice owners—aren't wired to sell. Financial services practice owners strongly prefer to keep on working and holding on to their predictable, low-overhead, sub-40-hours-per-week practices (common for many mature, fee-based practice models).

Over the years, as we talked to many advisors and asked about their future plans, a common refrain emerged that we've taken to calling the "rolling five-year plan." Here's what we've heard over and over again: "In five years or so, I'll sell this thing and walk away." But as it turns out, three or four years later, it's the same plan: "In five years or so, I'll sell this thing and walk away, but not quite yet." The only thing that consistently changes the course is a serious health issue, which often brings everything to an untimely end, at which point it is often too late to sell what's left of the practice for any real value.

To be certain, selling an independent financial services or advisory practice has been and remains an excellent choice for many advisors, and we are happy to help you accomplish that goal. External transitions are a successful and reliable exit strategy. But consider this: The average age of a selling advisor over the past 10 years has hovered between 58 and 60 years of age, not 65 to 75 as most people think. These sellers are usually individuals who have decided it is time. They decide there is more that they want to do and fewer rules and regulations that they want to deal with, and they go out and start a jazz band, teach math at an inner city school, and yes, sail around the world.

So, having thoroughly made the case for selling as a viable exit strategy, why isn't this a more common form of finding a successor or someone to replace you as the primary advisor? The answer provides an important key to the power of succession planning and building a valuable and enduring business. The primary reason is cash flow. Advisors are married to their take-home pay—the money that they take home every month, every year to support their lifestyles. Selling the practice and living off the invested proceeds pales in comparison to "five more years of income" and then selling. But indefinitely postponing both selling and succession planning has a very predictable result—it kills the practice, and, left unchanged, that is what will happen to 99 percent of today's independent advisors.

I guess at this point it is okay to pile on the bad news and get it over with. From the perspective of an independent broker-dealer, custodian, or insurance company, the only thing worse than being told that more than 90 percent of their advisors' practices won't be selling, ever, is that the data are clear that those same practices will stop growing and will decline in production and value for about 10 years *before* they die out. But that is exactly what our data indicate is happening, though even basic observation is capable of confirming this obvious fact.

As an industry, from top to bottom, we need to turn this around and become the leaders of all professional service models in succession planning—in building multigenerational practices that recruit and retain the best of the next generation. Fortunately, all the tools are in the toolbox with which to build a great succession plan; the solution has evolved and it is ready for full implementation, so let's get started. With this book, we have set some rather ambitious goals. We intend to do the following:

- Help you define your goals and set up a realistic timetable
- Help you understand the concept of equity, including how to use it to build a business
- Show you how to set up a proper continuity plan to protect what you have built
- Help you learn what's involved in a succession plan and how to set one up, step-by-step
- Show you how to perpetuate your income for the rest of your life
- Prepare you to handle the inevitable bumps in the road on your long journey
- Explain how to create a legacy

MIND YOUR OWN BUSINESS

One of the first steps in the planning process is to take ownership of your work—not so much thinking like an owner of your practice, but thinking like a business owner. There is a big difference between owning a practice and owning an enduring and valuable business. Remember the first day of being an independent practice owner? Remember the thrill, the excitement of owning what you do, and being responsible for more things than you ever thought you could handle? All that in exchange for a first-year paycheck that wasn't so great? Throughout it all, through the good times and bad, through all the lessons that were learned the hard way, there was the promise of something greater. What was your goal? What was it that you wanted to build? Was it simply to increase your take-home pay, or to make your own decisions?

Owning your own business is a big deal. It is not for the faint of heart or for those who prefer to avoid risk and hard work. And it is not for those who are comfortable placing limits on their aspirations or their income. For most entrepreneurs, being a business owner is about control and choice, and being an independent financial services professional offers all this and more.

But being an entrepreneur in this industry is still mostly about selling and producing. Right now, at this point in this young industry's time line, the primary skill set of an independent financial professional is that of being a salesperson, and even if you disagree with that blunt assessment or believe that it does not apply to you, take a look at your compensation system.

The predominant reward system for advisors in this industry is a revenue-sharing arrangement, also called a commission split or an eat-what-you-kill approach. Every owner or advisor or producer has one primary job: to produce revenue. Production becomes not only job number 1, but job number 2 and job number 3 and job number 4. Everyone makes a grab for the top line and is rewarded for doing so. Building the business rarely enters into the picture, especially since there is no bottom line to work with.

This revenue model is not without merit. As we've said, it works great for a wirehouse. It works great for an independent broker-dealer or custodian or insurance company. Follow the same formula and you, too, will be successful and make lots of money. Want to grow faster? Get more people and pay them to produce more revenue. But is that really your model? Is that what you want to build, and will it serve you well one day in the future when you start to slow down? As an independent, you are your own enterprise. You own what you do and you have some choices to make in the process.

As an independent owner, production of revenue is job number 1. We get it. But as a business owner, you already know from experience that the day is long and the task list includes many, many more duties and responsibilities than just producing revenue. You have to fix the copier, install software on the new computer, answer the seven voice mail messages (which include a complaint or two), lay out the coming year's marketing plan, hire a new receptionist, and so on.

As an owner of a small business, you do not have the luxury of limiting your expertise to one thing, such as production. Why in the world would you pay next-generation advisors like owners for doing just one thing like producing revenue? If you're going to build an enduring business, you have to move past this point. Making the jump from a practice to a business means that you have to create a bottom line and then restrict the rewards of that bottom line (the profits) to those who invest and actually do the work of an owner; production alone does *not* entitle anyone to a share of the profits.

When it comes to key staff members, or even a son or a daughter in a family business, forget the tired notion of trying to get them to think or act like an owner—either you're an owner or you're not an owner. Ownership involves risk and work that doesn't always come with an immediate reward. Ownership means taking a risk that you may never be paid, even while you place a second mortgage on your home, even while you work seven days a week and watch your earnings go down due to the economy, even while you take two steps backward for every step forward, especially in the early years.

Create a path and an investment opportunity and see how it goes, but stop pretending that great producers are "kind of like owners." They're not. But they probably should be, if they're willing to take the risk that ownership entails in order to obtain the full benefits.

Are you wondering what the difference is between a practice and a business? You won't have to wonder for long; we'll provide you with the specific definitions. In sum, a business is about more than just you, it is about more than just production, and it is about more than just making money during your career; it is about building something greater than the number of producers you can gather and share revenue streams with. Building a business is about empowering those beneath you to achieve more, as a group, than you could ever do as a single entrepreneur—and not being afraid of helping them achieve that goal.

As it stands, succession planning in this industry is too often not a matter of what you'd like your business to do for you and your clients, or what you need it to do for you and your family, but what you've limited it to doing by lack of knowledge, incorrect assembly techniques, and starting the planning process way too late to fix anything. We're going to help you change all that.

THE OPPORTUNITY AT HAND

It requires a great deal of boldness and a great deal of caution to make a great fortune, and when you have it, it requires ten times as much skill to keep it.

—Ralph Waldo Emerson

In October 1999, Boston College's Center on Wealth and Philanthropy published a study by Paul G. Schervish and John J. Havens entitled "Millionaires and the Millennium: New Estimates of the Forthcoming Wealth Transfer and the Prospects for a Golden Age of Philanthropy." The study predicted that over the 55-year period from 1998 to 2052, a minimum of $41 trillion will pass from one generation to the next in the United States. This particular estimate was based on a low-growth (2 percent) scenario; a 3 percent growth rate would provide for an estimated $73 trillion transfer of wealth, while a 4 percent growth rate (the highest used in the study) would result in an estimated $136 trillion transfer of wealth. In sum, the greatest transfer of wealth in the history of mankind lies before us—before you.

Serving the creators of this wealth are the many independent financial services professionals and advisors. Given an average maximum career length in this industry of 25 to 30 years, it is obvious that the only way to preside over this transfer of wealth is to create a business with multiple generations of ownership designed to serve multiple generations of clients—an enduring business. But that is exactly what is not happening in the financial services industry, at least so far.

The lifetime of a business may not be perpetual, but it should certainly be designed to outlive its founder's career length, especially a business that is designed to help individuals plan ahead for the protection, growth, and eventual transfer of their wealth. In this respect, the wirehouse or captive advisory models have a significant advantage over their independent competitors. The current generation of independent investment professionals must evolve beyond the simple one-owner, one-generation practice model and into a business built to serve and to thrive for multiple generations.

The future of the independent financial services and advisory industry is not going to be shaped by consolidators, banks, or even competition from CPAs and estate planners; it will be shaped by investment professionals who, in partnership with their broker-dealers, custodians, and insurance companies, develop businesses that are more than the sum of the talents and production levels of their advisors and producers. Businesses built to endure and stand on their own and to attract and recruit their own talent based on their own strengths and benefits offered—that should be the future, but it has yet to be written.

For all the advisors we've worked with, all the voices we've listened to over the phone, and all the valuations we've performed, there is one undeniable fact about the independent industry: Most advisors go it alone each and every day. Most advisors are forces of one, not about to be lapped, consolidated, or otherwise rendered obsolete before their time. Ironically, if the Great Recession taught us anything, it is that today's independent advisors are survivors. Still, your careers will come to an end, as will a lifetime of work, if you do not take the time to master the skills of building a business. Instead of dropping the curtain and walking away, let's consider this the opportunity that it is, and start to build something special. With this book, you have the tools to succeed in this venture.

CHAPTER 2

How to Start Creating Your Succession Plan

When considering your succession plan, your actual starting point depends on what you want or need your business to do for you, your family, your staff, and your clients. Remember that the goal of most succession plans is *not* to remove you as the founder and put you out to pasture; the goal is to build an enduring business around you that can provide an income stream for life while providing leadership and mentorship to a team of internal successors while gradually handing off the reins over a period of 5, 10, 15, or even 20 years if the planning process starts early enough.

DEFINING YOUR GOALS

There is a high degree of customization for every succession planning strategy. In fact, over the past 16 years, we've never done any two plans that were exactly the same. Plans are kind of like a set of blueprints for your dream home. While the building materials and assembly techniques for most homes are very similar and the tools consist largely of hammers, saws, drills, and the like, every home is as unique as the person(s) it is constructed for. That's how it is with designing and developing a succession plan—it is a plan that starts with you, and your goals and dreams.

The problem with setting specific goals for a succession plan is that you've probably never done this before. You've walked through other people's homes and gotten some great ideas while figuring out what you like and don't like, but most advisors never get to see another advisor's actual succession plan. It is very difficult to decide what you'd like to do if you don't understand what is possible, what is normal, and what won't work— these are all tasks that this book will help you with. In fact, we'll actually show you pictures of various plans, what we call "succession planning schematics" or blueprints.

Many advisors have an idea of what they'd like from a succession plan, such as creating a legacy, cashing out, spending less time in the office, and/or maintaining current cash flow for as long as possible—all valid starting places and ideas to build on. Some advisors think of their buy-sell agreements (that are triggered on death or disability of the owner) as their succession plans. This approach can transfer assets and relationships, but having to die to implement any kind of a plan maybe shouldn't be your first choice! We can do better than that.

So, while your plan will almost certainly contain a number of very personal goals, here are a few of the more common and general succession planning goals we hear on a weekly basis, beginning with the most popular:

1. Develop a strategic growth plan that doesn't center on the founder's skills.
2. Create a practical and reliable continuity plan that will protect the value and cash flows of the practice.
3. Provide for income perpetuation to the founder for his or her lifetime.
4. Transfer the business to a son, daughter, or other family member in a tax-efficient manner.
5. Accommodate an on-the-job retirement while never fully leaving the business.
6. Work for another couple of years and then sell and walk away or fade away.
7. Merge with another business as a means of growing, protecting, and optimizing value.

All these goals can be accomplished under the right circumstances, but some do require more time than others. While selling to a third party doesn't take a lot of advanced planning, for example, selling internally does. Executing an internal ownership strategy can easily take 10 years or more. Perhaps the best question to ask isn't "When is it time to start?" but "When is it too late to accomplish your goals?" In this chapter, we're going to help you answer those questions and more.

Rethinking Your End-Game Strategy

Conventional wisdom suggests that an independent financial professional should choose, at some point in his or her career, between an internal succession plan and an external sale to a third party or a merger with a third party (as in a peer, a competitor, a bank, or a CPA firm). That's wrong. Forget it.

The smart plan includes both options right out of the gate, but always starts with the internal ownership transition strategy—even if you have only two people, including yourself. The task is to design and develop a plan to guide your journey. If your internal plan doesn't work out to your satisfaction (and that is always a possibility), an external sale to a third party becomes your fallback strategy.

PLAN A	SELL INTERNALLY
PLAN B	SELL EXTERNALLY

As you're now aware, more than 90 percent of advisors will never sell their practices—at least not in the conventional sense—because the value they covet is not that offered or paid for by an outside, third-party buyer; the value most advisors are after is cash flow, the money they take home every year from work that is rewarding, as well as a client base that is more appreciative than not. Advisors would simply rather keep working, and keep earning the income that supports their lifestyle; the truth is, most advisors need to keep working because their lifestyles demand it. And even if they didn't, the stream of income multiplied by "five more years of working" is a more powerful incentive than selling for a lump sum and living off those proceeds.

So make selling your practice plan B, and face the music—there is less than a one-in-10 chance this is going to happen. You're not helpless in this matter, of course; plan B is mostly within your control unless and until it is triggered by death or disability (the purpose of a continuity plan) or you choose the attrition route and there is nothing left when you're done with it. Later in this book we'll help you better prepare for these possibilities. In the meantime, let's shift to plan A and start to figure out what that might look like for you and your stakeholders.

Setting up an internal ownership track (which is what powers a succession plan) provides for a stronger and more stable business, which in turn provides higher value in the future regardless of your exit strategy. It can also provide excellent protection against the founder's short-term or temporary disability. Attracting, retaining, and properly rewarding next-generation talent is an essential step in moving beyond a typical practice to a more valuable business model and solving these problems.

As a business owner with a succession plan in place, you can lead and continue to participate in the business you've founded for decades to come if you build an enduring and transferable foundation. In addition, the effective value received can be upwards of six times the trailing 12 months gross revenue, based on the starting point for the plan (including equity and profit distributions)—a fair return on your investment of time and leadership. The final, effective value derived by selling equity incrementally in a growing business is significantly higher than a sale to a third party, but only if you build the foundation to support this process—something to consider as you formulate your goals. Do you want to do this? Are you up for it? It is okay if the answer is "Maybe not," because honest answers provide for better goal setting and more accurate planning. Just understand that most plans can be designed around your preferences if there are sufficient time and resources.

We ask every one of our planning clients what "retirement" means to them. The answers are mostly the same. Retirement for an entrepreneur rarely means a hard stop; usually it is a gradual, on-the-job retirement from five or six days a week down to four days, down to three days, and so on. But that works only if there is next-generation talent to back you up, and a plan to tie it all together; otherwise, it is called attrition and any value other than cash flow will evaporate by the time most advisors call it a day. Worse, if a health condition or an accident cuts your plan short but doesn't kill you, the cash flow is gone, too, even when you need it most, and there probably won't be any funding to cover the equity value.

In the end, it all comes down to what you want and need from your business, and how much time there is to build the foundations and to implement and adjust the plan. That's why figuring out when to start is so important.

Determining a Precise Starting Point

Most advisors who do embark on designing and implementing a succession plan are starting about 10 years too late. Every year, we work with several hundred advisors to set up formal, long-term succession plans, and these founding owners tend to be around age 60 when they start the planning process—not too late for a successful plan to be designed and implemented, but not optimum in terms of maximizing results and having the broadest array of options.

So when should you start developing your succession plan? The short answer is, start the succession planning process by age 50, plus or minus five years. The longer answer is that it depends on what you want your business to do for you in the future. For the one advisor in 10 who actually will sell and walk away, start the planning process about three to five years before you think you're ready to pull the plug, and monitor your equity value annually to make sure you're not already in attrition mode and bleeding off value before you sell; at some point, practices do become unsalable.

One of the best ways to determine when to start your succession planning process is to first plan your "workweek trajectory." In other words, instead of focusing on either how much money you need from the business, who might possibly comprise your succession team of next-generation talent, or how much ownership you're willing to part with during the initial stages of your plan, look instead to something much simpler and closer to home—forecast the amount of time you would like to physically spend in the business in the years to come. We use a graph like that in Figure 2.1 to determine an advisor's current workweek trajectory and goals for the future.

Start the trajectory with an accurate assessment of the average number of hours you now spend in the office or working diligently on office-related matters from home. Then plot how many hours you'd like to be working in five years, 10 years, and so on. What is your goal and what would you like your business to do for you? Just to provide you with a level of comfort before we proceed, we tend to assume that perpetuating your current income level is a part of the succession planning process, even as you slow down and reduce hours in the office, so this important consideration isn't being ignored. We plan for it every time.

Some workweek trajectories bottom out in future years, which signifies a hard stop at some point in a career, and an end to at least the income stream for the founder, but most don't. Most advisors plot a gradually descending workweek plan but level it out at about half time based on what they're used to as full time. One of the benefits from a well-structured succession plan is the ability to elongate your career by reducing the hours and the stress, and by shifting the things you don't like to do to your up-and-coming succession team. Extending the length of your plan means a longer period of income and profit distributions along the way—in other words, a more lucrative retirement whenever and however that event might unfold, by working less. But to make that all happen, you need a good plan.

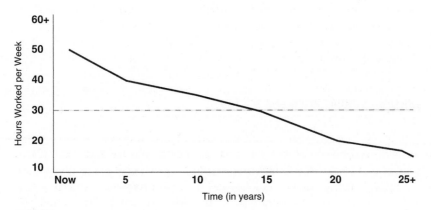

FIGURE 2.1   Workweek Trajectory

You'll notice that there is a horizontal dashed line drawn at the 30 hours per week level. We call this the "30-hour threshold." The 30-hour threshold provides an important lesson for founders and succession planners: There are more ways to shift control, or to lose control, of a small business than just selling shares of stock in your corporation, or membership interests in your limited liability company (LLC). Independently owned financial services or advisory practices are notoriously intolerant of absentee ownership, especially when the compensation systems in place are revenue-sharing arrangements or any form of an eat-what-you-kill system.

Working less and less as you get older makes sense and to some extent is inevitable; in fact, plan on that happening. But at a certain point, about 30 hours per week on average over the course of several years, attrition will begin to take its toll. Here is what happens.

Over time, the equity value of your business, specifically the value of your ownership and shares of stock, can be reduced to the value of the assets, namely the client relationships. As you work fewer and fewer hours but remain the owner of 100 percent of a practice, especially one with a revenue-sharing or other eat-what-you-kill compensation structure, the very portable assets of the business can factually transfer to the advisor who regularly sits in front of the clients and helps them. The result is that, at some point, the assets and client relationships take on more value than the founder's stock (or ownership interests in an LLC), and the next-generation advisors suddenly have something to negotiate with—something powerful and valuable that they control without having to purchase anything. In other words, the clients will follow the junior advisor across the street if he or she elects to go that way.

Accordingly, you should start your formal succession planning process five to 10 years before you break the 30-hour threshold. If you do, there is no reason why you can't enjoy the lifestyle the business provides, perhaps for the rest of your life, along with the cash flow and the gratitude of your clients and your family.

BUILDING A FOUNDATION FOR SUCCESS

In fairness, almost every small business has to start out with a singular focus on revenue—you have to make money to survive and make it to the next year. The art of production, learning how to give great advice and/or sell appropriate products and services, is how advisors make a living, and for that reason "revenue strength" is the principal component in determining the value of a privately held, independent financial services practice.

| REVENUE STRENGTH | ENTERPRISE STRENGTH |
| External Transition | Internal Transition |

FIGURE 2.2　Balancing Revenue Strength and Enterprise Strength

Building revenue strength is almost intuitive to advisors, but rarely is it balanced by "enterprise strength" (see Figure 2.2).

The basic goal of every succession plan we design and implement is to build an enduring and transferable business. Making the leap from a one-generational practice to an enduring business is not actually the role of succession planning; a succession plan builds on top of a durable business foundation and creates a plan for the transition of ownership and leadership. Building the foundation should be an entirely different process, one that needs to start closer to age 40 for the founder if it is to achieve maximum success with a staff in place and trained to support the business; ideally, with time and information, the process will begin upon day one of the business.

Most of the succession plans we design and build, however, require that we first retrofit the practice with the foundation and structures needed to build upon to create an enduring business model. So, if you are reading this book and you are under age 50, forget succession planning for a moment (yes, those are brave words in a book about succession planning!), and focus instead on building the foundation of a business that can provide you with a great succession plan when the time comes, such as when you're over age 50! It will happen, trust me. In the meantime, your energy is better spent building the foundation of a business that is valuable, uses the correct compensation system, and is set up to attract and retain contributors to your business who can eventually be included in your succession plan.

If we could boil this section down to one sentence, here it is: *Structure your business and its organizational, entity, and compensation systems so that there is no way for an individual to do well unless the organization succeeds as a whole.* There you have it: the secret of building an enduring business model. But how do you do that?

There are three areas that you will have to address and improve upon, some immediately and some more gradually over the coming years:

1. Your organizational structure
2. Your entity structure
3. Your compensation structure

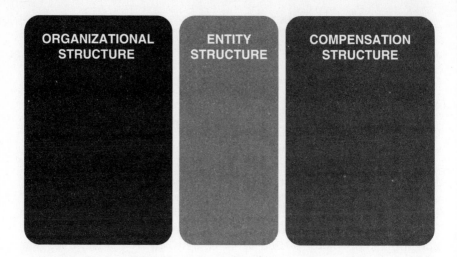

Understand that there is a fair amount of overlap between these areas, as will be evident from the instructions and explanations provided here. This overlap functions more like reinforcement rather than redundancy, adding strength to your business and its sustainability over time; but it also creates the possibility of weakness if you do just one or two of these right and fall flat on the third. You have to do all of them with at least a modicum of success, and this book will provide a lot more information on each in the pages that follow.

Advisors, like business owners everywhere, have a lot on their plates. It is easy to get overwhelmed when you look around and think of all the things you have to do and try to figure out where the time and energy will come from. Instead of looking around your office as it sits today, think about it this way instead: Imagine your business at twice its current revenue or value—what will the company be doing differently? What will your role be in that organization? What people will you need to add to get the business to that level and to take some of the load off you? If you're not retiring in the next 10 years, plan around such a goal and think long term as you hire and build—but plan before you hire and build.

FACING YOUR BIGGEST CHALLENGES

My first foray into the world of the independent financial services professional occurred more than two decades ago as a securities regulator. While employed by the Oregon Securities Division, I discovered and investigated one of the largest financial fraud cases in the state's history. But on my first day at work I was handed a copy of the Oregon Revised Statutes (ORS) and the Oregon Administrative Rules and told to write up a set of proposed rules for transitioning an independent practice. The Internet was still a thing of the future, so I learned the old-fashioned way: I picked up a copy of the Investment Advisers Act of 1940, ORS Chapter 59 on securities regulation, and the Securities Exchange Act of 1934, and I read the material, page by page; then I started asking questions.

Of my more experienced colleagues, I asked: "Can independent advisors sell their practices when they're ready to retire?" and the answer was: "Of course not; there is nothing to sell." I then asked, "So what is the point of writing up rules for transitioning their client base?" The answer was in the ballpark of: "Just follow the rules the wirehouses use—that's how everyone does it. There is no discernible difference between the two models." And that answer has stuck with me ever since—just do what the wirehouses do. Of course, that answer and its logic were wrong, but it permeates the culture of advisors to this day.

We have the opportunity to talk to thousands of independent owners and their staff members every year, and almost everyone still has some tie back to the wirehouse side of this industry. Some of you started your careers there and learned the ropes before jumping to the independent side. Others learned from a boss, a parent, or other mentors who received their training from one of the large, captive models. The wirehouse industry provides the foundation and education for most of today's independent financial professionals and advisors. To be sure, there were many, many good lessons to be learned and brought over to the independent space—but there were also some lessons and tools that simply do not apply to those who own their own business.

Over the past 20 years or so, independent ownership is *the* story in the financial services industry. But independence has an Achilles' heel—the practices die off with no one to succeed the founder. Too many practices aren't even capable of generating a successor because of how they are assembled. The culprit is the use of wirehouse, employee-based compensation and reward systems that make production and sales achievements the pinnacle of a career. Not to say for a minute that these venerable institutions don't do a lot of great things for their clients and this industry, but there is simply no need for these folks to learn how to build an enduring and transferable business—that is not a necessary task under the wirehouse model.

In the independent space, building a business would seem to be the pinnacle of most careers, and it will be just as soon as independent professionals discover the most powerful and lucrative tool they have: equity. Equity is the value of the business separate and apart from the cash flow and compensation paid for work performed. It isn't that equity is struggling to get a foothold (it's not), but in this young industry,

70 percent of the professionals make less than $200,000 a year, and the immediate value they care about is cash flow; with little or no infrastructure, nothing they do even remotely looks or feels like any kind of business, and it isn't.

The problem, however, isn't limited to small practices or new start-ups. The independent professionals and advisors we work with that have annual production or gross revenues of greater than $5 million, even $10 million, almost all use some form of revenue-sharing arrangements or an eat-what-you-kill system that rewards sales and production tied to the top line, not the bottom line. "Fracture lines" are built into the practice model as individual books or practices are built in an environment that starts out collaboratively but most often ends up creating competitors. And advisors do this over and over again as if it were the most normal and natural thing in the world—which it is on the captive side, but Dorothy, you're not in Kansas anymore.

It is time to dispense with obsolete practices and incorrect building tools and to recognize that the world of the independent advisor is different from being in a wirehouse. Building an enduring and valuable business should be the goal of every independent professional with annual production or gross revenues of $500,000 or more. It is time to stop "owning a job" and get to work, building efficiently and effectively with the proper tools and for generations to come. Some of the biggest challenges you'll face in doing so lie in discarding what you've been taught is normal and right.

The Persistence of a Job Mentality

Correctly structuring compensation at the ownership level is a critical element to building a valuable and enduring business. Ownership-level compensation cannot be determined by a chart or a survey or even benchmarking data; at this level, the common mistake is to focus on the question of *how much* an owner should be paid, instead of *how* an owner should be paid. Independent advisors start this part of the planning process by seeking answers to the wrong question.

The compensation system most commonly utilized by independent financial professionals in this industry is some form of a revenue-sharing or commission-splitting arrangement. Revenue sharing is an easy and seemingly low-risk payment system to implement—certainly, on the surface, easier than hiring a bookkeeper and setting up a payroll service to generate a W-2 wage and withholding system. But the risk and true cost of a revenue-sharing arrangement become increasingly apparent the more successful the younger advisor becomes; any value other than the share of revenue typically belongs to the individual advisor responsible for building the book.

Instead of building businesses that evolve and improve from one generation to the next, advisors in this industry build one-generational practices, and subsequently rebuild them from scratch with each new generation of owners largely because of these eat-what-you-kill compensation systems. For that reason, jobs and practices that last for just one generation of ownership are plentiful; multigenerational businesses and firms are rare. The goal of a practice owner is one of production, and production equates more directly with cash flow than it does with equity.

In the independent sector, if your goal is to build a valuable and enduring business, then your focus should be on a team of advisors working together, compensated for contributing to and supporting a single enterprise, rather than building individual books and subsequently leaving with the clients and related cash flow they generate when the time is right.

Revenue Sharing: Heads They Win, Tails You Lose

Let's examine this premise. You hire a 32-year-old advisor (we'll call him Bob) with a newly minted certified financial planner (CFP) designation and a small book that may or may not follow him, but he is fully licensed (or registered as an IAR) and ready to go. You agree to a small base salary for one year, credited toward the payout structure, which is a 50/50 revenue-sharing arrangement. Bob turns out to be a complete and total failure. He couldn't sell a space heater to an Eskimo or create a financial plan that looks out past the end of the week. You let him go. You saved the costs and complexities of setting up a payroll, and you didn't pay for what you didn't get; but did you win? What exactly did you gain in this arrangement?

The best argument is that you cut your losses and on that point we'll concede. You definitely did that. But you lost a year or more in the effort, you're a little older and thinking about slowing down yourself, and now you have to start over with a new hire. So let's rewrite history and explore this from a different angle.

Bob instead turns out to be one of the best professionals you could have hoped for. He comes in early, he stays late, your clients love him, and most of his clients followed him. He produces $250,000 in gross revenue (or gross dealer concession [GDC] under Financial Industry Regulatory Authority [FINRA] rules) by the end of his second year, and all indications are that he'll double that by the time he has five years in with you. What exactly have you gained in this scenario?

Well, you get 50 percent of everything Bob produces, so that's $125,000 a year by the end of year two. That's a good thing. Bob takes the same amount of money home as his reward, a good payday for him as well. Of course, Bob hasn't had to spend any money on desks or chairs, a computer or a customer relationship management (CRM) system, a phone system, the office space, or a computer network or the staff to make all these aspects of a business come to life, but you did. So you take your half and you pay the rent, the staff, the light bill, and other expenses, and then you take home what's left. You own half the cash flow, halved again after expenses, but what about the equity—the value of the book?

After year five, Bob does indeed reach his goal and now produces almost $500,000 in top-line revenue per year. About 70 percent of this revenue is recurring. You decide to make Bob a partner in your business and offer him the opportunity to buy in, but Bob astutely asks, "What about my book? Do you want to buy what I've built or exchange it for an equivalent amount of stock?" Those are really good questions, and we hear them almost every day. You own part of the cash flow, while Bob owns all the equity. Bob controls the assets, and those assets (the client relationships) are portable. They may not all follow Bob as he walks across the street and hangs out his own shingle, but they could, and therein lies the strength of Bob's negotiating position.

This example illustrates the concept that, as independent advisors, there are two kinds of value: cash flow and equity. This is a critical distinction that separates an independent practice from a captive or wirehouse practice.

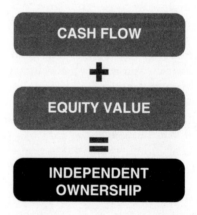

The point is that setting up a revenue-sharing arrangement or any form of an eat-what-you-kill payment structure is a losing proposition for the founder or actual owner, unless you own your own independent broker-dealer or custodian, a wirehouse, or an office of supervisory jurisdiction (OSJ); don't emulate these models for any other reason. Remember that most of those models are worth far less, per dollar of revenue generated, than your own enterprise. If the next-generation advisor fails, you lose. If the next-generation advisor succeeds, you have to buy what he or she has built and pay for it with the stock or ownership interests of your own business, or risk creating a competitor, and you lose again. Is cash flow alone, after expenses, worth that cost?

Think about this from the eyes of the next generation. When younger advisors are hired into a practice with no future of its own, a practice that is tied to the life or the career of its single owner, the very natural tendency is for them to build their own practices or books. Said differently, if there is no single enterprise to invest in, they start building their own practices and that is exactly what is happening in this industry. Acknowledging that is the first step toward building a business of your own that works for you.

Fracture Lines!

Revenue-sharing arrangements and other eat-what-you-kill compensation structures seriously undermine the effort to build a valuable and enduring business. Practices with more than one producer or advisor are being built with fracture lines from day one. Consider the diagram in Figure 2.3. In this example, Advisor A, who is 62 years old, is the 100 percent owner of an S corporation. He hires and mentors Advisor B, who is 42 years old, and years later, Advisor C, who is 36 years old. Advisor A provides his younger associates the bottom half of his client base and all new client referrals that are below his minimums or who are just not a good personal fit. This fee-based practice has a value of just over $1,000,000.

Four years later, when Advisor A is nearing retirement and is faced with a sudden and serious health condition, he decides to sell the business and

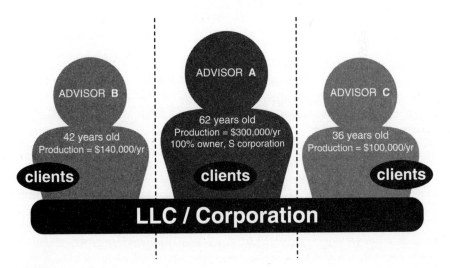

FIGURE 2.3   Fracture Lines

turns to Advisor B. Advisor B is interested in being the buyer, but doesn't want to pay for his own book, and certainly won't pay anything for Advisor C's book. When Advisor A looks outside the firm, a third-party buyer materializes and offers $1.6 million for the practice, but there's a catch. Advisors B and C must sign noncompete, nonsolicitation, and no service agreements, and/or formal employment agreements with restrictive covenants so that the buyer knows they won't interfere with or impede the buyer's ability to control and retain the acquired client base—except that they won't cooperate. And why would they?

All of a sudden, Advisors B and C's zero ownership positions are worth something—quite a lot, actually, as the junior advisors now have veto power over the value of their own books, cumulatively about $500,000 to $600,000 in value. The mistake most founders make is that they ask us to value the combined cash flows and think that they own and control 100 percent of the equity. How could they control 100 percent of the equity value when they or their practices don't control 100 percent of the asset base? This isn't one business; it is three separate practices. The fracture lines were built in from the first day Advisor A hired each junior advisor and paid him using the industry standard revenue-sharing arrangement.

This common example provides the junior, nonshareholder advisors with control over the assets (the client relationships) even though they haven't invested anything into building their own businesses: no lease of office space, no phone system or computer network, no employee payroll. All these things are provided through a revenue-sharing arrangement from Advisor A, who was willing to accept cash flow in exchange for the control and value of the assets in each junior advisor's book. This is not an anomaly; this is why there are so few sustainable businesses in this industry.

The junior advisors, in turn, enjoy cash flow with minimal investment and risk—what we describe as "owning a job." But what happens if Advisor B or Advisor C gets hit by the proverbial bus as he steps off the curb at the end of a hard day? He owns nothing that is transferable. His family receives little or no value even with the typical revenue-sharing continuity agreement, and, with no infrastructure, the relationships he controls are gone in a heartbeat.

These built-in fracture lines take a single practice with multiple advisors and create multiple books that, cumulatively, are unsalable and therefore end up somewhere between worthless and worth less (than they should be). Creating a competitor is never the goal, but unfortunately creating an equity partner and investor, at least for 99 percent of advisors, hasn't been one of the goals, either. It's time to change that, and as an independent owner, you have the perfect tool for the job—equity.

EQUITY—A POWERFUL BUSINESS-BUILDING TOOL

Independent financial services professionals enjoy a distinct and important advantage over captive advisors: They have two kinds of value to work with to reward themselves, to build with, and to use to attract and retain next-generation talent:

1. Cash flow
2. Equity

Equity is the key—it is what separates a one-generational job or practice from a more valuable and enduring business. Equity has always existed in the independent practice model, but it was more theoretical than practical up until the point where it could be accurately and affordably measured. Once measurable, equity required a proving ground, a place where the measurements could be tested and adjusted against a network of third-party buyers. Would buyers actually pay the values sought by sellers? The short answer was an emphatic "Yes!" Today, there is a 50-to-1 buyer-to-seller ratio, which supports a strong value proposition and a margin of error on FP Transitions' Comprehensive Valuation Report of plus or minus 4 percent.

Let's start with the most familiar form of value—cash flow. Independent owners pay themselves from the cash flow generated by the work they do, the products they sell, or the advice and guidance they provide; its flexible, it's fluid, and it's fun. Owners know how much money they take home every month. By the end of the year, with help from their bookkeeper and/or CPA, owners know precisely how much money they made, and how (wages, bonuses, draws or distributions, 1099, or W-2). And by comparing income statements, an owner knows how much more (or less) he or she made this year compared to years past, to the penny.

The equity value of a practice or a business or a firm is similar in many respects to the benefits of the cash flow, and different in a few key aspects. Equity exists because of the competitive open marketplace that generates a 50-to-1 buyer-to-seller ratio. It's kind of like owning a house; if the demand is high, you have value; you don't have to sell your house to have value, and that is exactly how it is with a financial services or advisory practice or business. Most advisors will never sell, but most have significant value, and that value is a powerful building tool when integrated into a long-range planning strategy, because equity is what next-generation owners actually invest in. (See Figure 2.4.)

Just as cash flow has its measurement tools, so too does equity. Equity is determined by a formal and professional valuation (not a multiple of revenue or earnings, which is like measuring the sufficiency of your cash flow by what's left in your checking account at the end of the month!). Annual

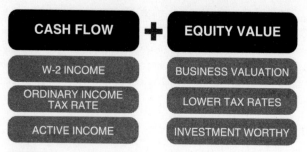

FIGURE 2.4   Business-Building Tools

valuations, an essential part of the equity management process, provide a library of valuation results, creating a historical record that is of great interest to key staff members, new partners, or recruits being offered a current or future ownership opportunity in the practice.

Equity grows from year to year in most cases, certainly over a span of time if the business is growing. Equity has the ability to provide a regular income stream to the founder or founders of an independent financial services business with proper planning. Cash flow has the advantage of being immediate; in an established practice or a business with recurring revenue, it arrives predictably, and the overhead to generate it is more or less predictable as well. Cash flow is the part of a practice that founders are willing to share. Equity is what next-generation advisors invest in, and buy from an informed founding owner with a solid succession plan. Equity is what provides the return on investment advisors make, and it serves as the means for many of those investments as well.

A frequent mistake made by advisors in the independent financial services industry is to equate cash flow with equity or practice value (or to link the two in a linear fashion with a fixed multiple of something times the trailing 12 months revenue). To this end, doubling the amount of cash flow in an incorrectly but commonly structured practice model often results in little or no change or improvement in the value of the practice. In other words, if value is created and retained by individual advisors, it makes little difference whether you surround yourself with two, three, or 10 advisor/producers—you might make more money in the short term as cash flow, but you will build almost no business value in the long term and there will be nothing for next generation advisors to invest in. And when you stop working, by fate or by design, the cash flow stops, too; and, with no enduring or transferable business value, the practice dies.

Measuring equity and using the value of the business as the primary determinant for growth is important because equity not only is a reflection of the cash flow and revenue generation capacity of a business, it also demands an assessment of the underlying foundation that supports the business's ability to grow and deliver services over time. Sustained equity growth directly impacts wages, benefits, profit distributions, and the ability of the business to maintain these functions from one generation to the next—a business of enduring and transferable value.

VALUING A FINANCIAL SERVICES PRACTICE

What creates value in an independent financial services or advisory practice? At its most basic level, value lies in the client relationships. In the earliest phases of the open market for financial advisors, most if not all of the value rested in the client base and the associated revenue. Even the language of the day referenced this characteristic, referring to the sale of an advisor's book, rather than the sale of a business. In this context, the supporting structure of services and staff, as well as other licensed professionals, was considered of secondary importance to the cumulative assets under management waiting to be transferred to another caretaker.

Valuation techniques have evolved to the point of being able to assess accurately the cash flow potential of a practice's client base, as well as the risk elements in transitioning that client base to another advisor or business. But the newest valuation techniques factor in more than just the clients and their revenue, adding infrastructure to the equation, what we call "enterprise strength"—the number of licensed employees who remain through a transition, the nature of the referral channels, and the level of technology in the practice, among other things. In other words, current industry-specific valuation methods consider the business elements as well as the details of the client base to ascertain value.

This approach mirrors exactly what is now happening in the evolving financial services marketplace. Astute and experienced buyers are seeking out advisory practices that have more evolved business structures, and they are paying higher value for these businesses. Accordingly, the valuation process itself can provide guideposts to owners looking to increase business equity.

The continual use of practice valuations can also help practice owners monitor the equity built or lost from one year to the next, rather than just monitoring fluctuating cash flows. In fact, obtaining an annual valuation is one of the most beneficial strategies for growing a business, as investment professionals who have their practices valued annually tend to keep equity management in mind through every business decision. And don't forget: Equity value is likely the largest number that you can add to your personal financial statements of net worth. That is an important consideration even from the aspect of a next generation, minority owner who is part of your succession plan.

There are a number of ways to place an accurate and authoritative value on a professional services business, including those in the financial services industry. Accepting that every valuation is an estimate until a buyer accepts and pays the price, the important questions can quickly be reduced to these:

- How accurate is a given valuation approach?
- How much does it cost to obtain an accurate valuation?
- Since almost no buyer pays all cash in this industry, how do the deal terms affect the valuation opinion?

Without positive and affordable answers to these questions, many practices and businesses in this industry would have no choice but to use a rule of thumb approach. Fortunately, there are good answers and at least a couple of well-accepted approaches when it comes to determining the equity value of an independent financial services practice or business.

In the financial services industry, it is relatively easy to discern a valuation multiple—at least in hindsight. Looking back over the past five years, the multiple paid for every dollar of recurring revenue (management fees and insurance renewal commissions, or trails) by third-party buyers ranged from a low of just under 1.5 to a high of almost 3.0. The multiple paid by third-party buyers for every dollar of nonrecurring revenue ranged from a low of about 0.2 to 1.7. That means that for the average fee-based practice or business in this industry, the range of multiples is from roughly 0.2 to 3.0. So go ahead and guess. You'll be wrong, but by how much?

Let's put this in perspective. If you have $125,000 in gross revenue or GDC and you're wrong on your valuation guess by just 20 percent, you'll cost yourself less than $40,000. If you own a practice worth closer to $1 million, the margin of error, in terms of dollars, will easily hit six figures. Given that most accurate, professional valuations used by advisors cost less than $2,500, it seems almost silly to belabor the point. Obtain a formal valuation as the first step in your planning process. If you're thinking of selling and walking away (or fading away), the same rule applies.

The goal of a professional valuation is to approximate closely a given business's fair market value. Fair market value has been defined as the price at which a property or asset passes between a willing buyer and a willing seller, with neither under any compulsion to buy or to sell, and both with knowledge of all relevant facts. Of course, where less than the entire ownership interest is being acquired, discounts may be applied to reflect the lack of control or lack of marketability.

Traditionally, a formal business appraisal uses a standardized format and one or more of these valuation techniques:

- Asset approach
- Market approach (multiple of revenue, multiple of earnings before interest and taxes/earnings before interest, taxes, depreciation, and amortization [EBIT/EBITDA], or comparable sales)
- Income approach (present value of discounted future cash flows)

Many of the tools of traditional business appraisals are poorly suited for valuing a dynamic, fluid, and personality-based business like an independent financial services practice. The least appropriate of the traditional valuation approaches is the asset-based approach. This method is not applicable to financial services practices, because there are relatively few tangible assets (computers, copier machines, and file cabinets) in such a model. In contrast, the real value of a financial services practice lies in the strength of the client relationships and the transferability of those relationships, which, in turn, generates the future cash flow of the growing and enduring business.

At the other end of the spectrum, the income approach analyzes the earnings of a given practice or business; it is "bottom-line, looking up." This method uses a going-concern approach, assuming that the firm will continue into perpetuity. Earnings-based appraisals work best for larger businesses and are well suited for those businesses of approximately $20 million or more in value. This approach also finds a practical application in support of an internal ownership track where advisor/investors purchase a minority interest of stock in a financial services or advisory business. One challenge with the income approach lies in trying to accurately and consistently define what income is.

A second and more serious problem with the income approach is its cost. These valuations are accurate and very useful, to be certain, but they tend to cost between $10,000 and $35,000, depending on the circumstances, the purpose of the valuation, and the appraiser's skills and credentials. At this cost level, the income approach becomes problematic when used by next-generation advisor/investors to track the value of their investments and to consider buying additional stock from year to year.

The market approach, which is the primary methodology of FP Transitions' Comprehensive Valuation system, determines the value of a financial services practice by comparing it to similar practices that have been sold in a competitive marketplace. It is "top-line, looking down." This approach is intended to answer two specific questions:

1. What will a buyer pay for this income stream in a competitive, open market environment?
2. How will a buyer pay the seller the determined value? (That is, what are the deal terms?)

The analysis in the Comprehensive Valuation system is based on the standard currency of the independent financial services market, that of gross revenue (or gross dealer concession [GDC] under FINRA rules). This top-line approach reflects the common practice of buyers in the competitive open market, and makes comparisons from one practice to another far more accurate and consistent.

There is an assumption in the financial services industry that the skills of the buyer are fungible, and that, within reason, a professional can take over the practice and render approximately the same level of service and generate an equivalent level of client satisfaction. This assumption works because of the size of the marketplace. With a sufficient pool of talent to draw on, successful and experienced financial professionals can be found who have reasonably similar levels of education and experience. As such, it can be assumed not only that a buyer with the requisite skills can be found for a given practice, but also that many buyers can be found that possess the necessary and complementary skills.

This result shifts the focus of valuation almost completely to the client base being acquired and the revenue stream that results, and not how the services are delivered, nor the cost efficiency of the services, nor even whether the practice provides a unique service in the community. The seller is simply transferring the client base, and therefore a valuation analysis is principally focused on the revenue potential of the client base being transferred.

FP Transitions' approach is unique in terms of taking into account critical factors in assessing the strength and durability of the revenue streams of an independent financial services practice or business (see Figure 2.5). The first step is for the system to assess the transition risk for the subject practice. The next step is assessing the strength of the revenues of the subject practice, referred to as cash flow quality. The last step in determining value is to apply a market-driven capitalization rate to the adjusted GDC or gross revenue. This is the process that firmly links the valuation to market reality by applying capitalization rates that are keyed to the type of practice, its size, and, geographically, where in the country it is located. It should be noted that, as with the adjustments to transition risk and cash flow quality,

FIGURE 2.5 Valuation Indexes

none of the individual assessment factors tend to be large, but rather result in incremental adjustments to value and, in sum, produce results that closely mirror the reality of the marketplace as we see it every day.

The indexes of transition risk, cash flow quality, and marketplace demand were first introduced to the independent financial services industry in a 2008 white paper commissioned by Pershing, LLC, entitled "Equity Management: Determining, Protecting, and Maximizing Practice Value." Here is a closer look at some of the essential, underlying elements in FP Transitions' industry-specific valuation approach that will help you better understand what drives value in the independent space.

Recurring versus Nonrecurring Revenue

Because the value of a business is based on the assumption of a continuing stream of revenue into the future, it is important that the analysis take into account the revenue sources—specifically, what proportion of the revenue is recurring versus transaction based. Fee income is the most important contributor to cash flow quality, as it represents recurring cash flow, which, in turn, is among the most predictable and durable of the revenue streams produced by a financial services practice. Recurring revenues also are the most important revenue streams to a potential acquirer or successor, and hence these fee-based revenues usually generate the highest interest and value. From a valuation perspective, these revenue categories form an important starting point for determining value.

Recurring revenue is one of the most important single determinants of value of a financial services practice. Revenue produced through management fees or trails is ongoing and reasonably predictable, and highly sought after by buyers. In the case of insurance renewal commissions, or trails, these are considered only to the extent that they can be transferred to a buyer. Most insurance trails are restrictive in terms of their transfer. While the assessments used in the FP Transitions' Comprehensive Valuation system are applied to both recurring and nonrecurring revenue, more weight is placed on the recurring revenue component.

Transactional revenue is more elusive and difficult to predict. Transactional revenue does have a value, but it is essential to be able to show the propensity for additional revenue in the future and during the buyout period. Factors like the practice's historical revenue, rate of revenue growth, length of surrender periods, and quality of the relationship are instrumental in predicting this potential from transactional revenue. Due to FINRA/Securities and Exchange Commission (SEC) regulations, there are certain inherent limitations on the transfer and payment for transactional securities revenue streams from a buyer's perspective. For the insurance portion of a business, the client relationship index and client wealth index are used to predict the propensity for future sales from the existing client base.

Cash Flow Quality Factors

The quality of the revenue stream produced by an independent's practice or business is one of the key components of value. The cash flow quality index, introduced and used exclusively by FP Transitions, indicates the strength and durability of the revenue stream of a practice. These factors, addressed in the following paragraphs, include:

- Client demographics
- Asset concentration
- Revenue growth and new client growth
- Expenses

In looking at client demographics, statistically it is desirable from a value or equity standpoint to have the largest proportion of the clients in the 50 to 70 years of age bracket, while at the same time not having a large percentage of clients in the 70 years or older age group. This is a recurring trait we see in the largest and best-run financial services practices. The 50 to 70 years of age demographic is desirable because this group, in general, is not only at the top of their earning cycle, but also at the top of the saving cycle as well. Event drawdowns, such as purchasing a home, paying for college tuition, or making business investments, are less frequent in this age group, while the urgency of saving as retirement approaches becomes more salient.

The demographics of those clients in the 30 to 50 years of age bracket are also important, contributing to a developing revenue base. In our benchmark studies, this age group does not represent the majority or largest group of clients, at least in the most valuable practice models. The demographic group represented by those clients 70 years of age and older is often the wealthiest segment in a financial services practice or business. This group, however, is a less stable and less predictable source of long-term revenue as this group is subject to event drawdowns for trust disbursements, gifting, living expenses, health issues, and, of course, mortality. In practices where the majority of the clients fall into the 70-plus age group, the result would be a lower cash flow quality rating, and, depending on other related factors, usually a lower value.

Asset concentration is another consideration in calculating the cash flow quality rating; it is measured by assessing the total percentage of assets under management owned by the largest top 10 percent of a practice's clients (ranked in order of fees paid).

Revenue growth and net new client growth are significant contributing factors to cash flow quality as well and are measured separately. In our analysis, computed from information we collect from our clients, average annual revenue growth over the 2002–2011 period was 13 percent (evaluated as 5-year compound annual growth rates over the 2002–2011 period), with the middle 50 percent of the distribution growing by between 5 percent and 16 percent annually. The rate of revenue growth, however, is strongly influenced by market performance and therefore, by itself, is not a reliable indicator of the long-term strength of the cash flow. Net client growth, however, provides an excellent proxy for determining the future growth potential of the practice, as well as helping to determine the quality and strength of the referral channels and the client development systems that the practice has in place.

Practice expenses are taken into account as well in determining cash flow quality. Practice expenses are defined by the valuation model as (1) occupancy cost; (2) office overhead; (3) employee salaries, wages, and benefits; (4) marketing expenses; and (5) other or miscellaneous expenses. While the Comprehensive Valuation system does not use expenses to calculate net cash flows due to the variation in how expenses are classified and the difficulty of obtaining comparable statistics, the system does take into account expenses with regard to their impact on cash flow quality.

Transition Risk Factors

Transition risk is defined as the risk associated with transferring the clients, and hence the revenue stream, to a new owner or successor. A number of factors are involved in accurately assessing transition risk, including:

- Client tenure
- The tenure of the practice
- The willingness of the departing advisor to offer postclosing assistance

- The use of noncompete/nonsolicitation agreements
- Other factors such as remaining with the same broker-dealer or custodian, and a number of related continuity issues

The effect on valuation of the assessment of transition risk is to discount anticipated revenue transfer by the risk factor associated with the transition to a subsequent owner or successor. On average, experience dictates that in a well-structured, well-documented transaction, the level of transition risk is in the range of 5 percent, meaning that 95 percent of the clients and revenue will make the transition to the new owner. This number, however, has wide variation depending on the factors cited earlier, and therefore requires careful consideration in ascertaining the level of risk associated with a particular practice.

In general, the longer the client has been with a given independent practice or business, the less likely it is that the client will leave following an ownership transition without significant cause. Long-term clients are much more likely to stay through an ownership transition (whether to a third party or internally to other partners, managers, or employees); this is particularly true if the assistance of the selling owner has been structured into the transaction, or is part of an internal succession plan. This is a case of inertia working to the advantage of the transition.

A corollary determining factor for transition risk is the tenure of the financial advisory practice itself. The longer and better established the practice is, the less likely the clients are to leave the firm in the event of an ownership transition. A number of reasons may be attributed to this observation. In longer-tenured practices, the clients may associate the services more with the firm and less with any one individual, thereby making a change in ownership easier and more natural; longer-tenured firms also have acquired a marketplace reputation and position (often referred to as goodwill) that carries through in the event of a well-structured and professionally executed transaction.

The degree that technology is used in the office also factors into transition risk. In practices where there is a high technology level and where the owners have invested the time, money, and resources into the business component, the common result is that client contacts and tracking are more automated and in many cases more systematic as well. In these practices, the transfer of ownership often experiences less disruption than when the contact, processing, and office systems are not as highly automated.

Other ancillary factors that contribute to the transition risk assessment include the owner's willingness to grant noncompetition/nonsolicitation/no service agreements upon their retirement or exit, and having similar restrictive covenants in place with licensed employees.

Marketplace Demand Factors

Since value is ultimately determined in the open marketplace by what buyers will pay a seller for an independent financial services practice or business, it is important to consider the market demand factors that influence that value. There are several important factors in determining marketplace demand, including:

- The type of practice
- Geographic location
- Size

The first consideration, practice type, is categorized by whether the practice is transaction based, fee based, or fee only. It can generally be said that the higher the percentage of fee income, the higher the demand for the practice, and this is factored into FP Transitions' Comprehensive Valuation model. The caveat to this classification is whether the practice has a truly specialized niche, which, while often lucrative (and which may increase cash flow quality), can have the effect of lowering marketplace demand because the practice may appeal to a very narrow range of potential acquirers.

As for geographic demand considerations, it is simply a matter of a buyer's preference as to location. Practices that are located in highly desirable areas (which almost invariably means strong marketplace demographics) have higher demand than practices in rural or lower demographic profile locations. Geographic location has several other interesting aspects to consider. One is that when we list a fee-based practice for sale in Chicago, for instance, for $900,000, it will draw an average of 30 to 50 interested buyers from the general area. If we list the same practice for sale in Scottsdale, Arizona, we see an average of 30 to 50 interested buyers from the general area, and another 30 to 50 interested buyers from many of the colder-weather states.

Finally, the amount of revenue generated by an independent practice or business is an important consideration in determining market demand. This factor tends to be a matter of supply and demand; since the number of successful larger businesses that come on the market is far smaller than the number of lower-revenue practices, there is an asymmetry in supply, which tilts the demand equation in favor of larger sellers in the current marketplace.

Very small practices, those having revenues of less than $200,000, and businesses that have revenues in excess of $1 million per year also have a higher demand factor than those practices in between those revenue levels; one is easily affordable, and the other is more about quality. These demonstrated preferences over the years are accounted for in the market demand index, though it should be noted that the cash flow quality factors and transition risk factors may offset this advantage.

Addressing Insurance-Based Practices

The valuation of an insurance-based practice is different from any other type of valuation we perform. As a beginning, recall that the valuation of a financial services practice or business must address the following basics in order to provide an accurate assessment and useful business-building tool:

- The quality of the practice's cash flow
- The ability to transfer the clients and assets to a succeeding advisor
- The marketplace demand for what the practitioner has built

In addition to these basic indexes (cash flow quality, transition risk, and marketplace demand), an insurance-based practice requires further analysis to address the depth and length of client relationships with protection-based clients—issues that directly affect the probability, and profitability, of future revenue events. This additional level of study is referred to and quantified in the FP Transitions' Comprehensive Valuation system as the client relationship index (CRI).

There are many factors used to accurately establish a practice's client relationship index, but basically the CRI is divided into three primary subcategories for evaluation:

1. Client adhesion
2. Business systems
3. Client management

Separately, no one of these subcategories of the client relationship index significantly affects the overall adjustment to the valuation results of a financial services practice, but collectively, the sum of these factors provides a reliable guide to the overall quality of the client relationships and therefore the book's ability to generate future revenue events. Since the client relationship itself is the primary driver for predicted future conversions, a renewed focus on how this relationship is managed—now and in the future—is a critical aspect in establishing and even increasing the value of an insurance-based practice.

Impact on Value of the Payment Terms

The results of the FP Transitions' Comprehensive Valuation attempt not only to value the practice or business, but also to place the value within the context of commonly utilized deal structures and payment terms. The reason for this is that one of the most important components in a practice valuation in this industry is the structure of the transaction; practice valuations are inextricably linked to the deal terms. Comparing values or developing pricing for a financial services practice or business in the absence of understanding and employing the appropriate deal structure, which includes the tax allocations, can be very misleading.

The primary lending or financing source in this industry is the exiting or affected owners themselves or, for larger firms, the business enterprise; this is often referred to as "seller financing." (This is true for both internal and external transactions.) Seller financing, in turn, means that practice sales and acquisitions require a degree of cooperation and flexibility between the parties before the transaction is completed and for a period of time afterward, what we refer to as an "economic marriage."

Seller or company financing also means that retiring practice owners look to their successors for more than just the highest purchase price or the largest down payment. In a seller-financed transaction, buyers rely heavily on their own cash reserves or lines of credit for the down payment, and on seller financing to pay for the balance of the purchase price. In sum, it takes buyer and seller, in a cooperative effort, to make most transactions, internal or external, financially viable. This codependence often results in sellers choosing very highly qualified buyers (rather than the highest bidders) who are excellent matches in terms of practice style, business model, investment philosophy, and personality, which, in turn, often results in very high client retention rates, supporting the realization of highest value for the seller.

Deal structuring represents the apportionment of risk in the transaction between buyer and seller. The payment terms that underlie the determined value in our Comprehensive Valuation Report represent the most commonly utilized deal structuring approaches. The basic components used to finance a transaction or to structure a deal include a cash down payment, a basic promissory note, or a performance-based or adjustable note; earn-out arrangements are rarely used anymore and should be avoided by FINRA-regulated practices.

Profitability and Its Impact on Value

The value of an independent financial services or advisory practice has traditionally been driven by top-line revenue, as illustrated in the preceding pages. The ability to access that value in the succession planning process is driven by bottom-line revenue because of the internal ownership buy-in process. In other words, if you cannot consistently generate a reasonable profit, you cannot build a valuable and enduring business.

From the internal buyer's or investor's perspective, the business's profits serve a critical function in almost every case; profit distributions are the primary funding source for their buy-in. Profits are the source of money they will use to make the promissory note payments to purchase stock or an ownership interest from the founder or from the business itself. Profits also serve as a return on investment both for you (the founding owner) and for the incoming partners who are taking on the roles and risks of a formal business relationship. A business that distributes most of the incoming revenue on a revenue-sharing basis tends to have a nominal bottom line. In that common instance, next-generation advisors have little choice but to invest in a job, or building their own book, rather than your business; a paycheck or a share of revenue is the only way to earn a return on investment.

The point is, as a business owner, you have to find a balance between the top line and the bottom line if you're going to attract and retain collaborative business partners and next-generation advisor/investors. What is that balance? In our experience and based on our study of actual business models, we think the *minimum level* of profitability to sustain an enduring business model is 20 percent. Said another way, at least 20 percent of the business's gross revenue needs to make it to the profit line and be distributed to actual owners. In an S corporation, for example, profit distributions are tied to investment and risk, not to production. Profits serve as the return on investment for those who actually take the risk of investing in a business and creating the infrastructure necessary to endure.

The impact on value is this: When profits are lower than 20 percent, equity value, at least in the eyes of an internal advisor/investor, is reduced. As profitability increases, equity value is increased, as is the advisor/investor's ability to purchase ownership, which brings us full circle—the ability to access value is driven by bottom-line revenue.

Many practices, as they begin to transform into businesses, simply cannot achieve a significant level of profitability, and that is okay. Shifting from a revenue-sharing, one-generational practice is not supposed to be an overnight proposition. But work toward that goal. Succession plans have the added benefit of creating a long-term strategic growth plan for cash flow and equity.

Later in this book, we'll share an excellent strategy for achieving and even surpassing that 20 percent goal. Eventually, the profit line should be 30 percent or more to reward and attract ownership-level talent and to create a single, enduring business model. In terms of what the right profit level is for your business or firm, think of it as an investor would—after all, that is what you're trained to do as a financial services professional. As our valuation models become more sophisticated from year to year, as we learn alongside you, the profitability element will become more prominent and serve to provide a more accurate assessment of value from an investor's point of view.

For the methodology and the actual math on this concept, see the last two sections of Chapter 3, "Remodeling Your Cash Flow" and "Production Model versus Business Model."

PRACTICING EQUITY MANAGEMENT

The very notion of practice management means you're accepting limits on what you can build; managing a practice means it will die with you, or sooner upon your retirement. It means you've settled for building a one-generational income stream and then will leave your clients to figure out the rest. This isn't about semantics. Practices don't last, and this industry needs businesses that are built to last—enduring and transferable businesses.

As an industry, we need to start thinking bigger and smarter, and longer term. An industry of entrepreneurs is perfectly suited to doing just that, but to build a valuable and enduring business, you will need new tools and an approach that is focused on what makes an independently owned model different—equity. Say hello to the concept of equity management.

The term *equity management* was first used in 2007 in a research report published by FP Transitions. In that report, the concept of equity management was defined as follows:

> *Equity management is a concept focused on helping owners determine, protect, and optimize the value of their independent financial service practices. To accomplish these tasks, the process of managing practice equity necessarily includes building a business structure that can outlive the founding owner by integrating the next generation of advisory talent through hiring, practice acquisition, or merging.*

Professionally managing the equity in an independent business model can be condensed into five basic steps (see Figure 2.6) that maximize the value of the business for the individual advisor and create stability, predictability, and retention of clients and assets for the broker-dealer or custodian:

1. Determine and monitor business value.
2. Properly structure the entity, organization, and compensation systems.
3. Establish a continuity protection plan.
4. Generate strong and sustainable growth.
5. Transition leadership and ownership gradually as value is realized.

FIGURE 2.6   Managing the Equity in Your Practice

Managing equity is also intended to help you attract and retain next-generation talent, not just as producers, but as collaborative partners who may one day form your succession team. It is focused on helping practice owners monitor, protect, and realize the value of their life's work while providing for the long-term care and retention of the clients they serve. Most important, it transforms how advisors and their broker-dealers view a financial services practice, shifting from a vocation to a business of enduring value. If your broker-dealer's or custodian's practice management consultant doesn't talk to you about equity, or can't speak authoritatively on that subject, you're likely wasting your time. Equity management is how you transform a practice into a business—without it, you're simply talking about what size of practice you want to be constrained to.

In the end, doing what is right for the clients and doing what is best for the business are mutually dependent concepts. In fact, the only way to ensure that the value of a practice based on intangible assets (such as client relationships) will be fully realized by the founding owner is to provide for a seamless, gradual, and professional transition to a successor or succession team that has a clear understanding of the future needs of the clients, along with an enduring business and supporting staff. The creation and maintenance of this framework is called an equity management system.

Most of today's independent advisors are still focused on managing only cash flow, because that is the focus when running a one-person practice. The problem is that you need next-generation talent to invest their time, money, and careers to build on top of what you've started in order to create a valuable and enduring business, and advisors don't invest in cash flow. Remember, if the goal is to own a job, next-generation advisors can accomplish that almost anywhere. Equity is long term, and it shifts the focus from individual books to a single strong enterprise. But to get there, that equity has to be professionally managed and valued.

The starting place? Formal, annual valuations that determine equity value, that support a plan for growth and endurance, and that utilize the benefits of both cash flow and equity to reward and retain next-generation talent.

BUILDING PROFIT-DRIVEN BUSINESSES

Instead of building businesses that evolve and improve from one generation to the next, advisors in this industry tend to build, and subsequently rebuild from scratch with each new generation of owners, largely because of the eat-what-you-kill compensation system; this compensation approach, coupled with various FINRA rules and a production- or sales-first culture, leads to a sole proprietorship mentality and an emphasis on top-line production.

So how do you structure ownership-level compensation designed to build enterprise strength into a single, equity-centric business rather than growing several individual books of business under one roof? You start by shifting the focus to the bottom line: profits. Profits attract advisors who will work for you in exchange for an ownership opportunity and the ability to build on your foundation.

That seems like such a simple statement, such a natural and normal thing to do; almost every business that achieves any level of success focuses on profitability and sharing those profits with the equity partners. This step has not occurred for 99 percent of today's independent advisors because the thinking is still that of owning a job; a job doesn't have a bottom line, and it doesn't need one, because it has a short lifetime and no successors; it is about cash flow and cash flow alone. Shifting the focus from production to profitability is a critical part of the evolution of this industry; if this step isn't taken, almost every practice in this industry will work only as long as the owner and largest producer works. Collectively, we'll continue to build revenue mills instead of enduring businesses.

Profits—actual profit distribution checks issued by the business on a regular basis and restricted to those who become equity partners—will gradually shift the focus of the production mentality to thinking and acting like an owner. This will also attract advisors who wish to become owners. Remember, advisors currently have no need to invest in your business to obtain a share of revenue—they just show up and work. If the top line is controlled a little more tightly (not reduced, just controlled), and profits are paid out only to those who become equity partners, there is a great reason to take the additional step and to buy into the ownership circle. The risk has a reward, as it should.

Building a practice requires a focus on production or revenue generation; that's true in almost all small businesses. Building an enduring business requires past and future leadership to make the connection between a growing cash flow stream and the costs of such growth—in other words, a focus on the bottom line. In the independent sector, if the goal is to build a valuable and enduring business, the focus should be on a team of advisors working together, compensated for contributing to and supporting a single enterprise, rather than building individual books of business and then leaving with them and the cash flows they generate when the time is right. Structuring compensation to motivate ownership behavior and thinking is one of the keys to building a foundation for a successful succession plan.

CHAPTER 3

Transforming Your Practice into a Business

ASSESSING WHAT YOU HAVE BUILT

There is a clever use of terms and concepts in this industry such as describing the organizational structures of independent financial practices as "silos" or "ensembles." The basic notion is that a silo is a single book of business. The term *ensemble* is reserved for an actual business with multiple professionals who truly work together as a team, pooling their resources and cash flows, creating a bottom line, and then distributing profits to the owners of that business.

Silos can exist as part of a group, or they can exist as stand-alone offices, but effectively, they each have their own books of business regardless of the employment or compensation approach. Almost every one of the advisors we've ever worked with technically falls into the silo category. Even most of the advisors who have been around for 30 years or more and own fast-growing limited liability companies (LLCs) and call themselves ensembles are most often a group of silos. That has been our firsthand experience year after year. In fact, if we restrict our discussion to advisors with a value of $25 million or less, those for whom we have seen the data and that comprise most of the independent industry (at least in terms of a head count), we come across just a handful of true ensembles every year, out of thousands of engagements—that's it.

Still, these terms have been very useful in that they have focused attention on what you are building, and how you are building it. We couldn't agree more that correct structuring is critical to building an enduring business model; building the foundation is the prequel to the succession planning process. In his book *The Ensemble Practice* (John Wiley & Sons, 2013), Philip Palaveev made this statement: "When you arrive at the conclusion that you want to build an ensemble practice, you will find that hiring professionals with less experience and helping them grow into lead advisors is perhaps the most reliable and most available path to building an institutionalized, valuable, large firm." And he's absolutely right.

Let's build on that point and take stock of what you've accomplished to date. What have you built? One of the points we've consistently tried to make in this book is that, as an independent owner of what you do, you need different and more appropriate tools to work with than you've been given. To help you assess your position and to help you set your goals for the future more accurately and explain them to your stakeholders, we think a simple and intuitive shift in terminology will aid in the process. Consider these time-honored labels and the industry-specific descriptions that follow as guides for determining where you are today, and where you'd like to be five or 10 years from now:

- A job
- A practice
- A business
- A firm

We'll be the first to admit that these categories, as described in more detail next, will need to evolve and become better defined through actual usage over time, but here's a good starting point as to how these practical labels seem to break down in our experience:

A job exists as long as you, the advisor or financial professional, do it. You are independent, and you own what you do, for the most part. It is your "book." Whether W-2 or 1099, registered rep or investment advisor or insurance professional, it makes no difference— they can all fit equally well under this category. But when you stop and someone else starts, it's their job to do, not yours, and the cash flow attached to that job belongs in whole or in substantial part to the person doing the job. Of course it is about production; in fact, it is about nothing else. You work under someone else's roof, you own none of the infrastructure, you have no real obligations to the business other than to produce and get paid while taking care of your clients. The value of a job is tied almost entirely to how much money the producer or advisor takes home every year. There is no need for a succession plan or a continuity plan. You don't sell a job; you leave it.

A practice is more than just a job, often involving support staff around the practitioner and basic infrastructure owned by the practitioner (phone system, computers, customer relationship management [CRM] system, a payroll, etc.). But like a job, a practice exists only as long as the practitioner can individually provide the services and expertise. Practices are limited to one generation of ownership, and then someone else takes over—the practice is sold, or the practice is dissolved and the clients find their way to another advisor. Practices have one owner, whether formally in an entity structure or informally in terms of control over the client relationships (a book). The value of a practice typically is limited to about $1 million for a variety of reasons. The focus is entirely on revenue strength; there is little need for enterprise strength at this level. The primary succession plan is attrition, followed in second position by selling to a third party. Continuity agreements are rare, and life insurance is the primary solution, at least for the practitioner; the clients are on their own. There is little or no bottom line, and there doesn't need to be—no one invests in this model.

Here's where the bigger shift occurs. If the engine of production (the means of making money) rests solely or primarily in your hands and you cannot or will not change that dynamic, then you cannot build an enduring business that will outlive you; if that is the case, you own a job or a practice. A business, if that is your goal, is designed to make the founder replaceable at some point, even as the business continues on.

A business must have certain foundational elements in place: an entity structure, a proper organizational structure, and a compensation structure that give it the ability to attract and retain talent and additional advisors who enable this model to outlive its founder. A business is built to be enduring and transferable from one generation to the next and, as a result, is more likely than not to have an internal succession plan fueled by multiple owners from multiple generations. It operates from a bottom-line approach, and earnings, for the first time, begin to reward ownership and investment in the business. Many businesses still bear the name of the founder, and are working through compensation issues and the effects of revenue-sharing arrangements and are prone to creating competitors rather than collaborators, though they see the problem and are taking steps to try to address the challenges; the leadership is aware. Culture is increasingly important, though many businesses find that they may need to adjust and adapt to a different culture in the future. Continuity agreements are common and take the form of a shareholder agreement or a buy-sell agreement. The value of an independent financial services or advisory business ranges from at least $1 million up to about $10 million. A business gains its momentum and cash flow from revenue strength, and its durability and staying power by developing enterprise strength.

A firm is an established business, but in addition, it has achieved its value in excess of $10 million, at a minimum, by building a strong foundation of ownership and leadership by recruiting and retaining the very best people in the industry. A firm has multiple generations of ownership with key staff members vying for an opportunity to earn the right to become a partner and invest in the firm. It operates primarily from a bottom-line approach, and earnings are the measure of success, at least as important as production and growth rates. Profit distributions are the variable portion of an owner's compensation. Continuity agreements are a given, and the firm assumes the natural ability to weather the deaths or early retirements of its current leadership group over time. Collaboration among owners and staff is the rule. A firm emphasizes company-wide coordination of decision making, a group identity, teamwork, and an institutional commitment. The goal isn't to have the best professionals, but rather to have the best firm. Getting into a firm as a new hire is difficult. New hires not only must have the requisite skill set, but they also must fit into the culture and help it to thrive even as they work hard to support everyone around them.

In this book, from this point forward, when we use terms like *practice* or *business* or *firm*, those terms will be used specifically and within the context of the preceding definitions. We think the independent industry, in terms of a head count, fits into each of these categories approximately as illustrated in Figure 3.1.

Remember that while this is an industry with a relatively high average age, the typical level of production or revenue generation per financial professional or advisor at the major independent broker-dealers, custodians, and insurance companies is less than $200,000 per year—in many cases, much less. These professionals represent an incredible opportunity for business builders and for one-generational practices that need a second generation of talent to work with, mentor, and plan for, or even possibly just to acquire.

JOB (70%) PRACTICE (25%) BUSINESS (4%) FIRM (1%)

FIGURE 3.1 Four Industry Categories

It really depends on what your end game strategy is: What do you want your practice to do for you as you grow older? Do you want to build a business that can provide you with a lifetime of income and benefits and purpose? You do have a choice, if you build with the right tools and execute a sound plan with the right goals in mind.

A BUILDING PROBLEM, NOT A PLANNING PROBLEM

Advisors are not planning for succession and failing—they're not planning at all. And why would they? This is an industry of one-owner jobs and practices that were never intended to grow into enduring businesses (ensembles) or firms (super-ensembles as they are sometimes called). Planning alone cannot fix a structural issue, or worse, a series of structural issues. In fact, planning is not the problem; *building is the problem.* Once we collectively improve on the assembly methods and the tools, building valuable and enduring businesses will be as natural and normal as, well, providing long-range, multigenerational financial advice.

The wirehouse tools that have been borrowed as building implements by advisors place no value on business building and never had use for equity management in a cash flow only environment. As a result, most advisors and financial professionals don't even try to set up a formal succession plan—the thought never even occurs to them. If your goal is to progress from a job or a practice to an enduring business, you first have to build an organizational structure that can withstand the test of time. It isn't that hard to do, but it is best accomplished as part of a comprehensive plan, and ideally, well before designing and implementing your succession plan.

The common starting point for most advisors is a sole proprietorship model—a single advisor compensated on the basis of some form of revenue-split or eat-what-you-kill (EWYK) system, often working under someone else's umbrella. It resembles Figure 3.2.

This basic production-based or advisor-driven model is extremely adaptable and simple to establish and operate. If this model is set up with any type of revenue-share or EWYK (short for "eat what you kill") system, it is all about owning a job. Over time, as the competitive elements begin to

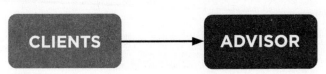

FIGURE 3.2 Basic Organizational Structure

FIGURE 3.3 Basic Organizational Structure

outweigh the collaborative attributes, advisors progress from owning a job to owning their own small practice, and it looks more like Figure 3.3.

Unfortunately, these common starting points are often mistaken as building blocks for larger, more sustainable business models; it appears to be as simple as doubling the cash flow by doubling the number of producers. In a wirehouse model or even in an independent broker-dealer, custodian, or insurance company, this is exactly the way it works and has for a long, long time. This results in a very common and predominant business structure in the independent financial services industry illustrated in Figure 3.4.

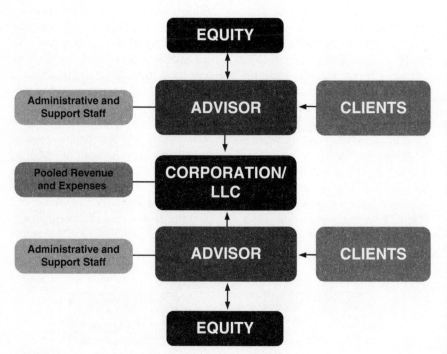

FIGURE 3.4 Individual Books Organizational Structure

This structure, for years generically described as a "silo model," is what we call a "practice," which is exactly what it is. A practice presents one common business name and structure to the advisor's clients and to the public, but the nucleus of the model, the corporation or limited liability company (LLC), has little or no value because only expenses are paid through its bank account. The value, or equity, is actually split between two or more advisors, each a separate, isolated production unit or book capable of taking his or her clients with him or her at any time.

From a buyer's perspective, the practice as a whole, certainly the entity itself, has no value. Adding more and more advisors to this model may increase total cash flow, but it usually does not change the resulting equity value of the founder's operations. This is the classic one-generational model that most advisors build almost intuitively.

The most valuable and enduring business models now emerging in the independent financial services industry are structured like Figure 3.5. This is a diagram of an independently owned business. It relies on a strong, centralized entity structure (LLC or corporation), which collects all incoming revenue (assigned from the receiving producer/financial advisors), pays out compensation (wages and benefits) for work performed (including production), and pays operating expenses. Controlling these top-line costs results in a bottom line, or profit distributions, and these profits, in turn, provide each equity partner with two essential results: (1) a return on the partner's investment, and (2) for new owners, the means by which to pay for that continuing investment. These results are why and how next-generation advisors invest in a more valuable business rather than building their own individual books.

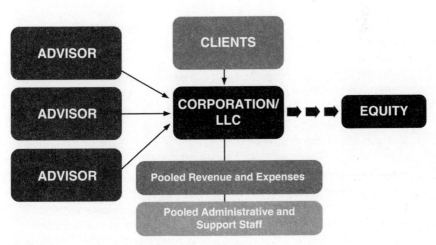

FIGURE 3.5 Equity-Centric Organizational Structure

So, why would a highly compensated producer who receives, for example, 50 percent of everything he or she brings in want to see a change in the organizational structure toward enterprise strength and away from revenue strength? Quite honestly, he or she may not. You didn't hire, train, or compensate your best producer to think like a bottom-line investor in your enterprise, and these folks often are paid as much as or more than most owners, with little or no risk of investment. Does that mean you have to jettison highly paid producers in favor of lower-paid, less capable producers? Of course not.

Our experience has been that about 85 percent of next-generation advisors/producers choose to physically and financially invest in being an equity partner in a business or a firm when it is offered. The rest? They already are paid and treated like owners; why sign a promissory note with a payment obligation and take the risk when the benefits of ownership have been freely offered for years? Discouraged? Don't be—there are ways to solve the problem, but the importance of your organizational structure cannot be overemphasized, or compromised. Here is another way to think about it that many of our clients have found useful and interesting.

A PARABLE

Consider this parable to better understand the organizational challenges most advisors face when trying to progress from a job to a practice, and ultimately to a business of enduring value over the course of a career:

> *Picture a bright orange life raft floating on a dark blue, storm-tossed ocean. In this durable, well-built small craft sits an independent financial advisor. Our advisor has a paddle for propulsion, the means by which to move the raft to safer or more prosperous waters. Our advisor has the means to collect and store rainwater for drinking, and fishing tackle to bring in food for survival—the craft literally is floating on a sea of food and fuel to sustain and propel its lone occupant. Our advisor also has a compass for navigation to guide forward progress along a chosen route; or, if preferred, our advisor will just drift as the winds and current dictate. Both result in movement.*
>
> *Over time, though the sea is vast, there are many financial advisors, and our advisor encounters other life rafts and other peers. Most of the time, they just pass by and coexist, easily and effortlessly competing for the same food supplies without much thought or concern. But in time, when the skies grow dark and the seas inevitably become more challenging and dangerous, behaviors tend to change. Instead*

of passing by each other, groups of advisors in their bright orange life rafts come together and form a group. Under the right circumstances, they'll lash their rafts together for safety and support and form a consortium of three or four, each sitting in their separate crafts, but inextricably linked together for the duration of the event.

During this time together, our financial advisors can explore various opportunities. Synergies may develop from the group, as the paddles are placed in the hands of the strongest advisors whose task it will be to propel the group to safety. The advisor best qualified to lead and navigate will take the compass and direct the group with a single vision and set of coordinated actions. And the advisor best suited to "hunting and gathering" will be charged with collecting water for drinking and food in order to sustain the efforts of his or her crewmates—each doing what he or she does best, contributing to the success of the group. But it is just as likely that each independent advisor continues to function as a separate unit, each eating what he or she kills and each reserving the right to cut the ropes and paddle off at any time and in a direction of his or her own choosing.

One of the biggest mistakes that financial advisors continue to make is to view this group of life rafts as the pinnacle of business growth and organization, or even as the goal—as it is in most practice management circles. The mistake is to think of this loose assembly of individuals and producers as a ship when in fact it is nothing more than a flotilla, quick and easy to assemble, and equally quick and easy to disassemble. The wirehouse model and even the independent broker-dealer and office of supervisory jurisdiction (OSJ) models we currently have are poor blueprints for building a valuable and enduring advisory business.

Later in this book, we'll talk about onboarding advisors with existing books and evaluating them as possible equity partners, and we'll differentiate their contributions in terms of what they impact: cash flow or equity value, or both. Here is another useful way to think about these kinds of issues. Your business is the ship, and the advisor with a small book is in a life raft. In year one of the onboarding process, allow the life raft to tie up next to your ship, and to enjoy the shelter and safety and convenience your larger and more stable vessel has to offer. Over time, if the onboarding process goes well, the advisor may leave his or her life raft and find a permanent place on your ship, or, if the process does not go well, the advisor can get back into his or her life raft and paddle away. That's what life rafts are built to do. Keep that in mind when you allow them to come alongside your ship and enjoy the efforts of your labors.

BUILDING YOUR SHIP

As we continue to evolve and fine-tune the more appropriate categories of building a job, a practice, a business, or a firm, let's apply the lessons to be learned from the preceding parable. What are the practical differences between a practice and a business?

The Life Raft Model	The Ship Model
About the best producers.	Group effort focused on the bottom line.
Focused on short-term goals.	Focused on short-term cash flow balanced with long-term equity growth.
Top-line revenue is the key.	Bottom-line profitability is the key.
The leader is the best producer.	The leader is the most experienced and capable advisor.
It's only about production.	Owners don't have the luxury of doing just one thing well.
The president's pay is based on production.	The president's pay is based on intelligence, leadership, and production.
One-generational.	Multiple generations of ownership create an enduring business.
Highly decentralized.	A valuable, central business owned by its advisors.
Eat-what-you-kill system is the norm.	Profit-driven culture, with profits available only to owners.
1099 compensation structure.	W-2 compensation structure.
Entity has little or no value.	Entity has all the value.
Value is centered in each producer.	Advisors are paid competitive wages for their work; profits are for owners.
Focus is on cash flow, not equity.	Focus is on shareholder value.
Revenue strength is very strong.	Revenue strength is balanced with enterprise strength.
Ownership exists, but only of a book.	Individual books are not permitted or rewarded.
A competitive environment.	A collaborative environment.
Nimble and adaptable.	Decisions are made collectively.

The Life Raft Model	The Ship Model
Continuity plan is a revenue-sharing arrangement.	Continuity plan is an enterprise agreement (buy-sell).
Nothing and no one to succeed the owner.	Succession plan is an integral part of the business plan.
Easy to assemble and disassemble.	Requires professional counsel (consultants, lawyers, CPA, etc.).

Building a ship is not for everyone, but more than 1 percent of the industry needs to do so—that is, needs to build enduring businesses. Think of it this way. If you own a job or a practice, you still need a continuity partner; you still need someone, someday, to step in and take over for you and to take care of your clients and their children and grandchildren, someone to pay fair market value and help you realize the value of one of your most valuable assets. Who better to do that job than the ship on the horizon? If you don't want to build your own ship, then steer toward someone else's when the skies become dark and the seas start to get rough; stay close to the ships out there. They can help in many ways and for generations to come.

RETHINKING YOUR COMPENSATION SYSTEM

In this industry, we are firmly convinced that the early generations are building life rafts by accident; it is what advisors with a wirehouse background or training think they're supposed to be doing, and honestly, they do it quite well. It is what advisors are told to do—that, and the simple replication of the models immediately available and obvious to every practice owner: independent broker-dealers, custodians, OSJs, branch managers, and the like. As you know, or as you're quickly learning, independent models are unique and they require special attention and special tools and assembly methods during the foundational building process.

Simply stated, revenue sharing is a terrible compensation system for advisors who want to build a business. Revenue sharing or commission splitting or any kind of EWYK system has a seriously detrimental effect on where the value, or equity, is centered—either in the enterprise or business itself (which can endure) or in the individual producer or advisor (which is unlikely to survive beyond the advisor's career). When compensation is tied exclusively to the top line, to gross revenue or total production, there is zero reason to aspire to ownership; there is no need to even hazard a glance at the bottom-line profits when you're paid off of the top line. This is a great deal for nonowner revenue producers; they take little or no risk, working only the hours necessary to produce revenue, and they get paid like an owner. But that is not how to build a business.

Here is an example from a group we recently worked with:

Mark and Katie Dickson, husband and wife, operated a fee-based business in Boston, Massachusetts. The value of their 23-year-old business was determined to be $2.5 million, enough to fuel dreams of a comfortable retirement. Mark and Katie were well-educated and experienced owners and collectively held the credentials of CFP, MBA, and CPA, and Katie was an OSJ as well. They were each 50 percent owners of an LLC taxed as an S corporation. Mark was 58 when we met him; Katie was 54. Mark and Katie had two key employees, Karl and Christina, and together, they wanted to design and implement a 20-year succession plan that would allow Mark and Katie to gradually retire on the job starting in their mid-60s.

The business was flourishing in most respects. In addition to substantial business value, Dickson Financial Partners, LLC, enjoyed a strong annual revenue growth rate of 14 percent (an average over the preceding five years), and spent only 38 percent of its revenue on overhead, not including owners' compensation. Payroll, occupancy costs, advertising, and information technology (IT) expenditures all benchmarked favorably against their level of competition. They performed annual valuations and tracked the growth of their equity value carefully.

Karl (age 39) and Christina (age 35) had no clients when they were hired by the business some years before. They were paid on a revenue-sharing arrangement and encouraged to "build their own books," and build they did. Whether with Mark and Katie's donated smaller clients or clients they found on their own, Karl and Christina managed to each build substantial recurring revenue–based books without ever having to invest or risk their own money in building an office or the infrastructure to support their production goals. And they didn't really have to worry about much other than production, which contributed to the high, sustained growth rate of the enterprise. Mark and Katie took care of everything from staffing to the phone systems to the IT issues, all in exchange for 50 percent of the revenue Karl and Christina produced. What Mark and Katie didn't pay attention to until too late was the equity value of the separate books.

Very recently, Mark and Katie were delighted to welcome Karl and Christina into the ownership circle and offered them each a discounted and seller-financed opportunity to become partners in the business, cumulatively buying 25 percent of their ownership in Tranche 1 of the plan. Karl and Christina were honored to be asked, but then responded with a series of unsettling questions:

- *"Why would we buy our own books?"*
- *"How much stock are you granting to each of us in exchange for the books we've built?"*
- *"Why would we want to become minority owners and at-will employees when we already own and control our own books and income streams?"*

Based solely on the production numbers, Karl and Christina would be 28.3 percent and 15.6 percent owners, respectively. Legally, they owned 0 percent of Dickson Financial Partners, LLC, but they were able to negotiate from a position of strength. They didn't want to leave and set up their own practices, and in the end they didn't have to. The deal got done and Karl and Christina ended up with 25 percent of the ownership of Dickson Financial Partners (worth $625,000), and a salary increase.

In the end, Mark and Katie realized that they had nearly made a $1.1 million mistake and created two potential competitors rather than two potential partners. Almost 45 percent of their cash flow could have walked away. Instead of selling a 25 percent stake in their business, they exchanged ownership for control over books they watched and enabled to be built.

Mark and Katie had managed over the years to retain 100 percent of the ownership and control of their LLC, but they failed to realize that they were slowly and certainly transferring away over a million dollars of that equity by saving money and using a simple revenue-sharing approach.

BALANCING REVENUE STRENGTH AND ENTERPRISE STRENGTH

Creating substantial and enduring value in a professional services business over the course of a career is a multifaceted challenge that will demand adjustments or improvements to a number of primary value drivers and support mechanisms. In addition to the more obvious elements of cash flow and incoming revenue, equity growth and management strategies also depend heavily on certain foundational elements such as the entity structure, the organizational structure, compensation methods and profit distributions, ownership tracks, and talent management initiatives—elements that speak to the strength and ability of an enterprise to grow and retain value over time.

By our estimate, 95 percent of advisors focus primarily or exclusively on revenue strength elements (the function of owning a job or a practice). The analysis of revenue strength covers an array of benchmarks, but focuses on the areas of revenue production, cash flow quality, pricing competitiveness, and efficiency.

Most independent financial services professionals and advisors understand how to build revenue strength (increasing the number of good clients and retaining those relationships); the challenge in making it to the enduring business level lies in building enterprise strength. *Enterprise strength* is a term we use to refer to a financial services business's legal and organizational structure (including its compensation systems)—in other words, its infrastructure. Are the necessary people, tools, and resources in place to build and support an enduring and transferable business over time? Can the business survive and prosper after its founder's retirement, death, or disability? Is it one valuable and enduring enterprise or many smaller, individual books that are just as likely to become competitors as collaborators?

Increasing both of these business components may seem like a sensible approach to increasing business equity, but the process becomes more problematic in achieving the end result over time. For example, increasing the number of clients and retaining those relationships as a business's leadership ages may require a substantial investment in staffing, training, and operational capacity, while pursuing a strategy of significantly increasing the revenue generated per client may require a change in culture, deliverables, skill sets, and operational systems. In either case, any increase in revenue that is accomplished by emphasizing one strategy or the other does not directly correlate to an equal or proportional increase in the equity value of a financial services business, nor its ability to sustain the rate of growth and to realize that value upon transition.

As a quick aside, ever wonder why there is such strong buyer demand for practices (today's buyer-to-seller ratio is 50 to 1)? Imagine if you were selling your home and had that kind of demand, in just the first 10 days! There may well be a number of good reasons, but consider this: The average buyer tends to be two to three times the size of the average seller. Big is buying small, and the motivation seems quite logical. Practices (see the previous definition) have an inherent limit on value because of how they're constructed. The highest value we've seen in the past several years, expressed as a multiple of gross recurring revenue, is just short of 3.0 times trailing 12 months revenue. The average multiple of fees or trails, as depicted in Figure 3.6, is

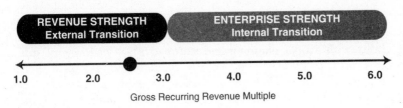

FIGURE 3.6   Gross Recurring Revenue Multiple

2.36 times trailing 12 months revenue. But businesses are more valuable; when sold internally, they tend to generate a much greater return, something in the neighborhood of 6.0 times trailing 12 months revenue based on the starting point of the plan, not including wages and benefits for the duration of the plan. Every dollar of revenue acquired from a practice and placed into a business with a balance of revenue strength and enterprise strength becomes worth far more.

Enterprise strength is not an elusive or difficult goal to obtain, if you know what you're doing, but it is not a building step many practice owners concentrate on. That's unfortunate, and that needs to change if your goal is to build a business of enduring and transferable value. Continue to focus on the concept of building a foundation for success before you begin the succession planning process. The three areas to focus on are your organizational structure, your compensation structure, and your entity structure. Having covered the first two earlier in this chapter, let's focus on the final and most straightforward of these three foundational elements: entity structure.

SELECTING THE RIGHT ENTITY STRUCTURE

Based on a steady stream of data from over 1,000 valuations per year, we know that eighty percent of advisors with values of $1 million or more are set up as an entity (S corporations or LLCs are the most popular models among advisors); above $5 million in value, close to 100 percent of advisors are structured as or make use of an entity. This is not a coincidence, as size and structure are directly related. Businesses require more than one person to run or administer them, and entities can accommodate that fact better than sole proprietorships or even teams. If you want to build a valuable and enduring business, set up a formal entity; that is step one in the implementation process and is a step best taken well in advance of designing and implementing your succession plan.

A sole proprietorship, or a corporation or an LLC with just one owner, will come to an end with the retirement, disability, or death of its owner;

it is built to die. A corporation or an LLC with multiple generations of ownership serving multigenerational client bases, on the other hand, has the ability with proper planning and staffing to last well beyond any one advisor's career or lifetime, and to create an enduring business with significant transferable value. This business value or equity, in turn, can support a variety of sophisticated succession plans for the founding owner and key staff members.

In this industry, we see the following structures used most frequently in the independent space:

- S corporation
- Limited liability company (LLC) taxed as a disregarded entity
- LLC taxed as a partnership
- LLC taxed as an S corporation

We come across some C corporations (occasionally as an LLC tax election) and a few general partnerships, but not in significant numbers. C corporations tend to be the entity of choice for older and larger firms (more than 20 years old and above $20 million in value—the 20:20 Club), but not so much for the practice models. We also set up and work with teaming arrangements that don't involve the use of a formal entity (usually due to compliance issues within the broker-dealer or insurance company). For the most part, S corporations and LLCs are the predominant choices by advisors.

One of the keys to building an investor-worthy business, or at least one of the more straightforward routes, is the use of a tax conduit, because it helps to channel money to the bottom line, a function that solves a number of important building and compensation issues. C corporations can work, too, but most advisors we talk to with this entity structure channel all of the cash flow out as compensation to avoid double taxation, providing no return on investment to next-generation advisors.

For those of you who reside in the realm of the sole proprietor model on the advice of your tax or legal counsel, understand that the benefits of proper entity structuring reach far beyond liability and tax issues. Establishing an entity structure and using it correctly can provide an excellent continuity solution as well as additional long-term strategic planning opportunities. Utilizing an entity structure along with ongoing, annual valuations to monitor equity can help retain and propel the next generation of advisory talent, which in turn can perpetuate your business while providing you with an income stream for the rest of your life. These common goals are almost impossible to achieve through a sole proprietorship.

One of the major advantages for owners who operate as an entity is the ability to transfer or sell small, incremental ownership interests to next-generation staff members, and create two or more owners of one financial services business. For example, a founding owner can set up an internal ownership track and gradually sell 5 percent, 10 percent, or 25 percent of the business to one or more key employees, paid for over many years in a series of tranches while retaining control, a process that is part of FP Transitions' "Lifestyle Succession Plan," explained below. The ability to create multiple owners in one enterprise, as you're learning, is the perfect antidote to the revenue-sharing, individual book-building approach that has created an industry of one-generational practices.

Note: Even though an entity cannot be paid securities revenues under Financial Industry Regulatory Authority (FINRA) rules, almost all independent broker-dealers permit advisors to contribute their earned revenues into a corporate bank account that pays expenses, including salaries. To be on the safe side, all owners should be properly licensed in order to participate in these structures and to receive profit distributions. Fee-only Registered Investment Advisers (RIAs) are a different matter, and are typically a little easier to work with in this regard. If you're FINRA licensed and you're not sure, check with your compliance department beforehand.

What You Need to Know

When deciding to form a business entity, attorneys and accountants tend to focus on two primary factors: (1) limited liability and (2) taxes. We'd add a third factor: (3) business perpetuation. For independent advisors, the limited liability portion of this equation is less important than for other business owners, because the prevalent liabilities are customer complaints and regulatory actions. The limited liability benefits of an entity structure will most likely not protect you in either case; this is why financial professionals often carry errors and omissions (E&O) insurance. However, limited liability can protect you against other potential business liabilities, such as creditors or accidents that occur on your property. Businesses with solid earnings histories may be able to execute an office lease with the entity being the lessee, rather than the principal of the business.

The tax issue is more complicated, but also more to the point of this discussion, which is why a CPA plays an important role in every succession plan we design. Most owners don't set up an entity solely for the tax savings. The broader issue is one of cash flow and tax efficiencies for both founder and next-generation owners (which we'll cover in more depth in the next section), but think of it this way. A sole proprietor has but one way to get paid, and then at the highest tax level on that ordinary income payment stream. An S corporation, for example, has two ways to pay its shareholders (wages and profit distributions), but three ways to build wealth when you also include payments to the seller of stock of that S corporation, especially over many years from a group of active next-generation owners (what we call "the succession team") as the business continues to grow, and at long-term capital gains tax rates. Again, the key is equity, and there are some incredible tax efficiencies that are a part of most succession plans and all of them benefit from an entity structure of some type.

The one factor that most attorneys and accountants overlook is the issue of perpetuation—the ability to build something that can outlive you. A sole proprietorship or a one-person entity simply cannot accomplish this task. You need a structure that next-generation advisors can take ownership of, very gradually over the course of a career. Entities are built to do exactly that.

In terms of selecting the right entity type or understanding what you currently have, start with this basic premise: Most advisors will benefit from a flow-through model, or tax conduit—think an S corporation, or an LLC taxed as a disregarded entity, a partnership, or an S corporation. Why does this matter? Recurring predictable revenue has more advantages than you may realize—it also provides recurring, predictable overhead, which means you can run the cash flow model on a leaner setting than just about any other professional services practice or business. In other words, you can take more money home because it is easier to know how much, or how little, you can leave in the bank account. Flow-through entities are not built to retain earnings. If you're a next-generation advisor looking for a way to pay for the stock you want to acquire, that is a very good thing because all future growth dollars in a properly structured cash flow model will stream to the bottom line (after expenses, of course), where they will be discharged in the form of a profit distribution check to each owner. For these reasons and more, most choices come down to a basic S corporation or an LLC.

Before we go into specifics on these two primary choices, it is important to understand that selecting the right entity structure isn't just about what's best for you right now or as you build your business; it is also about what is best for your future owners. It is all about building a sophisticated vehicle to help every owner build wealth by building a single, strong, equity-centric business. In the process, don't confuse complicated with sophisticated; you do not need one entity for every half-million dollars in revenue to build an enduring business. Keep your entity structure simple and understandable; later, we'll add and define a new and relevant term in this regard: *investor-worthy*.

If you're looking for a more direct answer and you're not yet in an entity structure, here it is: Choose the LLC. It can evolve with you and your business, and it can support virtually any succession plan you or we can design. It also can provide some important tax benefits when onboarding talent into an ownership position.

Limited Liability Companies versus S Corporations

Limited liability companies are relatively new on the landscape. Corporations have been in existence for hundreds of years, whereas LLCs did not come into existence in the United States until 1977. Despite the late start, almost 45 percent of today's independent advisors who have an entity structure have chosen the LLC format, and there are many good reasons for this choice. Lest you stop reading now and settle on the LLC as the best choice and be done with it, you're going to miss an important point: You have to learn to think in two dimensions to fully understand and utilize the LLC structure, and that's where the S corporation comes right back into play as an important consideration. For that reason, you need to understand how both models work.

LLCs are a hybrid that combines features of a corporation with the operational flexibility enjoyed by partnerships and sole proprietorships. An LLC is often a more flexible and fluid structure than a corporation, and it is well-suited for a practice that starts with a single owner and progresses to a business with multiple owners. An LLC has the unique ability to elect to be taxed as a sole proprietor (or disregarded entity), a partnership, a C corporation, or an S corporation; in other words, you get to choose your tax treatment. (Sadly, electing *no* tax treatment is not yet an option!) Further, an LLC with multiple owners or members that elects to be taxed as a partnership may specifically allocate each owner's or member's distributive share of income, gain, loss, or deduction through its operating agreement on a basis other than the ownership percentage of each owner or member, something an S corporation simply cannot do.

An S corporation must distribute earnings and/or losses according to ownership interest. For instance, if you have two owners, one who is a 75 percent owner and one who is a 25 percent owner, the earnings and losses *must* be divided 75/25. There is no exception. However, in an LLC taxed as a partnership, the earnings and/or losses can be split however the owners agree in their operating agreement. For example, if the ownership interests are again 75/25, the owners can agree to split the earnings or losses 50/50, or any other manner in which they agree, and they can change it from one year to the next as a matter of contract. S corporations allocate profits and losses as a matter of law. Although an S corporation has to pay distributions strictly according to ownership interest, owners can effectively adjust this aspect of the cash flow by paying compensation (think salary and bonuses) at their discretion.

Any person or legal entity can own shares (usually called units or membership interests) in an LLC, and there can be any number of shareholders (called members) or classes of stock or ownership, depending on the tax treatment. LLCs can have deductible employee pension plans for both owners and nonowners. In most states, LLCs taxed as a partnership lose their W-2 status and are subject to self-employment taxes.

S corporations are corporations that permit flow-through income taxation. Every corporation actually starts as a C corporation. To obtain S corporation status, the corporation has to file an election with the Internal Revenue Service. With an S corporation, you may be able to reduce some of your self-employment taxes by paying out profits in the form of distributions after paying reasonable compensation. This can save you significant amounts, depending on your particular circumstances, but you should discuss this carefully with your tax advisor because there are limits to the effectiveness of this strategy.

S corporations have restrictions on ownership that most LLCs do not have. Some of these differences include:

- LLCs can have an unlimited number of owners whereas S corporations can have no more than 100 owners.
- S corporations can have only one class of stock. LLCs, depending on the tax treatment, can have unlimited classes of stock or ownership interests.
- Non-U.S. residents can be owners of LLCs, whereas S corporations may not have non-U.S. residents as owners.
- S corporations cannot be owned by C corporations, other S corporations, LLCs, partnerships, or many trusts. LLCs are not subject to these same restrictions.

LLCs are not subject to the same formalities as a corporation, but it is very important for an LLC to have a proper operating agreement, especially in the financial services industry, where there are often additional rules for ownership. S corporations face more extensive internal formalities, including adopting bylaws, issuing stock, holding initial and then annual meetings of directors and shareholders, and keeping the minutes of these meetings with the corporate records. These formalities are requirements that exist even for one-person corporations.

In an S corporation, what you see is what you get. It is rigidly structured, it is predictable, and it is inflexible. Some owners consider those points to be detrimental, whereas others consider them advantages. Remember that in most succession plans, there is a distinct possibility that you'll be a majority owner and a minority owner at different points in time, depending on whether you're the founder gradually selling your ownership or a next-generation advisor gradually acquiring ownership. Having profit distributions set as a matter of law can be a positive feature, depending on which side of the fence you're on. In that way, S corporations have the advantage of being investor friendly. Twenty- and 30-year-olds who have never owned a business intuitively understand how stock ownership works and how it is taxed; LLCs, especially when set up as a partnership, are an entirely different matter.

LLCs taxed as a partnership offer a unique strategic advantage in this industry and in the context of building enduring businesses, however. Independent advisors tend towards building their own books, often right under their employer's roof. In the process we call onboarding, acquiring those books in exchange for an ownership position can be difficult and expensive through an S corporation, in terms of the taxes. Purchasing or acquiring an existing book in exchange for an ownership position (i.e., buying the book with stock of the corporation) results in ordinary income tax treatment to the owner/contributor of that book; the stock he or she receives is taxed at ordinary income rates, often as part of a cashless transaction. In this area, LLCs can have a distinct advantage because of how partnership tax law works.

So, LLC or S corporation? The answer is, for most advisors, both! And now that we have you thoroughly confused, let's clear away the clutter and get back to that bottom line. While about 45 percent of today's independent advisors who have an entity structure have chosen the LLC format, two-thirds of all advisors who have an entity are taxed as S corporations, half of them directly, half of them through an LLC tax election. The S corporation is the predominant tax structure to plan around in the independent financial services industry because it works and it is easy to understand and cash flow model.

If you're already an S corporation, you'll likely always be an S corporation; you don't need to change a thing in most cases. If you choose the LLC model, or have already chosen it, you have the ability to elect to be treated like a sole proprietorship, a partnership, a C corporation, or an S corporation, in sequence as your business grows—the best of all worlds. This goes to our earlier point of learning to think two-dimensionally in your entity plans: You file as one thing, and get taxed as something else. Most advisors who set up as an LLC will progress in tax treatment, one step at a time, from a disregarded entity to a partnership to an S corporation. Consider that assumption in your succession planning process; your next-generation owners will.

One last point: LLCs are far more complicated than S corporations, and not by just a little bit. That makes them more expensive to set up and to operate, and it means you're going to need professional help to do it. Don't even think of trying to set up an industry-specific LLC, designed to perpetuate a business beyond your lifetime, in this highly regulated industry using some online service or an attorney who doesn't know what FINRA stands for, or how an RIA handles cash flows. Building an enduring business in this industry is an exacting process. Do it right the first time, and build your business on a solid foundation with the right tools.

REMODELING YOUR CASH FLOW

In order to build an enduring business—something that can outlive you while providing a lifetime of benefits and income through your succession plan—an independently owned practice needs to be repowered with next-generation talent. In fact, as the value, cash flow, and complexity of the business grows, most succession plans involve not just one next-generation advisor, but a succession team with owners filling specific roles in the enterprise. As a founder, don't be afraid of this change. Embrace it, because it cannot unfold and it cannot be successful without your help; you're the cornerstone and will be for a long time to come.

To assemble this team, the founding owner has to be able to draw younger, talented advisors into the ownership circle and help them answer a couple of important questions: (1) "What am I investing in, and why?" and (2) "Where does the money come from to enable me to buy into the business and, one day, to buy out the founder or senior partners?" Proper cash flow modeling is the key to helping next-generation advisors invest their money and careers in the business in which they work, because it helps to create a bottom line or profit distribution in an LLC or an S corporation. Profit distributions, actual profit distribution checks issued several times a year to all owners, serve as the practical answers to those questions. Creating those distributions is one of the key steps in transforming your practice into a durable business.

In this book, we'll assume that all current and prospective owners are actively involved in the business, and are properly licensed or registered to provide services or sell products that generate revenue and help the business pay its bills and grow. In other words, succession planning in this industry tends to be about active ownership, not passive ownership. With these basic assumptions in place, the following is an explanation of how to create a bottom line or profits that attract and reward active, next-generation advisors.

Let's start with how cash flows through an independent advisor's S corporation (or an LLC taxed as an S corporation). Basically, there are two ways to get money out of an independent practice or business—wages and profit distributions. But there are three ways to build wealth from the same model: (1) wages (S corporations or LLCs taxed as an S corporation can and should pay W-2 wages to their shareholders), which include bonuses; (2) profit distributions; and (3) equity value.

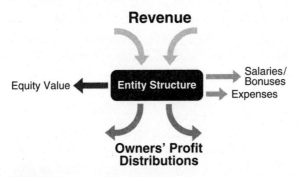

FIGURE 3.7 Cash Flow Modeling

The addition of equity or business value to the equation is essential and part of the business-building process, because the growth of equity has the lowest tax rate of the three wealth-building tools, and we're not talking about long-term capital gains rates. Think instead about the tax on the growth of equity in your business or, for comparative purposes, your home; you don't pay taxes on the growth of equity until the equity is realized. As a growth tool, as a building tool, equity is what separates an independent business from a wirehouse model. It bears repeating: If your broker-dealer or custodian's practice management team cannot help you address the equity component, then they're treating you like a practice and not a business. They're thinking small; are you?

Referencing Figure 3.7, consider the process step-by-step from an owner's perspective.

Step One: Collecting the Revenue

A properly constructed and valuable business relies on a strong, centralized entity structure that pays out competitive-level compensation (wages and benefits) for work performed. First, it must collect ALL incoming revenue from everyone who works under the same roof, and deposit every last cent of that money into the corporate (or LLC) bank account. This is a normal function in a fee-only, RIA model where a client can contract directly with the advisory firm; in a FINRA model, this can be a more challenging aspect as the money paid to the individual advisors must be assigned into the entity.

The point is, if revenue is siphoned off through a revenue-sharing arrangement or a commission split, *it does not count* toward the value of the business. That is the difference between cash flow and equity. That is also the difference between separate books and a single business with enterprise strength. All revenue belongs to a business, without exception, and is distributed as set forth in the next two steps.

Step Two: Paying Competitive Wages for Work Performed

Competitive wages at the ownership level are determined by relying on two information sources: (1) the producer/advisor's trailing 12 months compensation level and (2) operational benchmarks for practices or businesses of similar size and composition. As a general rule, however, no succession plan or business plan should start with a pay cut to a next-generation advisor who is about to become a new owner as part of the creation of an internal ownership track. Accordingly, determine what the competitive wage is for a particular role in a particular geographical area, but regardless, don't reduce take-home pay. Making the leap from a revenue-sharing arrangement to a salary and bonus structure is hard, but you don't have to do it all at once; we often include a tapering element in the planning process (as pertains to the compensation element) as you transform from a practice into a business.

Once salaries are determined, lock in the most recent level of compensation, and don't change it for the next couple of years—and that statement applies to all owners, including and especially the founder. (Most of the larger businesses and firms we work with do not reset or increase compensation every year—that is the function of profit distributions.) This creates a base-level compensation for the ownership team (check with your CPA to ensure that reasonable compensation levels are paid for tax law purposes if you're an S corporation or an LLC taxed as an S corporation). Over time, as the founding owner begins to reduce time spent in the office (the purpose of establishing the workweek trajectory), his or her wages tend to remain flat even as the business grows, a benefit of ownership and being the founder.

Alternatively, on occasion and depending on the circumstances and the planning parameters, the founder's wages can gradually be reduced as the founding owner works less, but only as he or she receives incoming payments from the succession team who are gradually purchasing their equity at increasing stock values—taking into account that these monies are received at long-term capital gains rates by the founder/seller. Connect the dots: As wages decrease or level off and as the business grows, profits will increase, triggering a faster buyout of equity from the founder at preferential tax rates—all excellent reasons why you should plan first, and thoroughly, before implementing your succession plan. There are a lot of moving parts.

As a result of this cash flow remodeling, the role of variable-level compensation is shifted to profit distributions—an element to be reserved for those who actually invest their money and careers into the building of a single, enduring business. It is essential that the founder pays at least competitive wages in order to attract and retain exceptional talent for the long term, but it is a mistake to overpay by a significant amount (which almost always occurs when you use a revenue-sharing arrangement or any form of an eat-what-you-kill system), thereby making an investment in ownership unnecessary by the employee or producer/advisor. Why invest and take a risk when a share of the profits automatically comes with the paycheck?

Step Two and a Half: Bonuses

The immediate push-back in a sales-based organization is that a pure base salary coupled with profit distributions does not properly incentivize employees to achieve the results needed to grow the company. If that is the case and you believe the company goals cannot be met without production-based compensation, then we suggest using bonus structures specifically targeted to the behavior that the practice is trying to encourage rather than simply tied to a blanket revenue goal or production from an individual. Using a bonus incentive tied to bringing on new clients or to increasing so-called share of wallet is better than using revenue-based splits or commissions, which often reward advisor employees for simply participating in a good market rather than achieving the goal of building value. By using appropriate base compensation combined with profits to the owners, bonuses gradually become a smaller component of an advisor's compensation package and one that serves more to focus on the right objectives while keeping things interesting and competitive among your junior advisors.

Step Three: Profit Distributions × 3

A flat, or at least a more flat, wage level means that after operational expenses are paid and a suitable reserve is on hand, all remaining monies as well as all future revenue growth (after expenses) will be channeled out of the pass-through entity structure as profit distributions to the advisor/owners. Remember, in an S corporation tax structure, profits flow to owners in direct proportion to ownership (i.e., a 15 percent owner receives 15 percent of the profits). Profits serve three distinct functions: (1) serving as a return on investment, (2) serving as the variable component of take-home pay (a very different and effective approach when compared to revenue-sharing arrangements), and (3) providing the means of paying for the equity being acquired from the founder. Again, those are the critical differences between a practice and a business; creating a bottom line is how you create and sustain an enduring and valuable business.

Flattening the founder's W-2 wages also means that the founder can't take out all the growing profits as a bonus to himself or herself. Instead, by paying those monies out as profits, an important business-building function is attained: advisor/owners learn to think like owners, focusing not only on production (which is still job number one), but on profitability as well. This structure reflects the philosophy that owners of small but growing businesses are not motivated only by a paycheck, but by the increasing size and share of their profit distributions, and by the growth in value of their investment (think shareholder value), or equity—three ways to build wealth as a business owner.

Obviously, in order for advisors to increase their share of the profits and to increase the amount of their variable compensation in terms of actual dollars, additional ownership must be purchased, and that is exactly the mentality needed to create and sustain the succession team. But there are two additional and easier ways that next-generation owners can increase their take-home pay as equity partners. One is to grow the top line—help make the business grow and take more and more of that responsibility on as a member of the succession team. The second is to watch the bottom line: How profitable is this business? How does it compare with other businesses of similar size and structure? What expenses can be cut without affecting growth?

Simply asking the questions is a step in the right direction for the next-generation team of owners—the succession team. But you have to get them to focus on production *and* profitability simultaneously; that is what owners learn to do. And owners learn very quickly, because production and profitability immediately and directly impact their take-home pay. The greatest failing of a revenue-sharing or eat-what-you-kill arrangement is that those compensation methods make the bottom line completely irrelevant to all but the founder, who alone, late at night, worries about the increasing overhead.

Step Four: The Investment in Equity

Building a practice requires a focus on production. Building a business requires past and future leadership to make the connection between a growing cash flow stream (production) and the costs of such growth (profitability); it shifts the focus to the bottom line. Having and distributing profits, a bottom line, attracts next-generation advisor/owners who can, in turn, provide continuity and longevity. At this point, it bears repeating: Structure your business and its organizational, entity, and compensation systems so that there is no way for an individual to do well unless the organization succeeds as a whole.

In general, here is a good formula to consider as a goal for the business you're building: About 35 percent of all incoming revenue should be allocated toward overhead (business expenses, not including ownership-level compensation); about 35 percent of all incoming revenue should be allocated to ownership level and advisors'/producers' compensation; and about 30 percent of all incoming revenue should find its way to the bottom line, to be allocated to profit distributions and accessible only by those who have invested in the firm and are shareholders or legal owners. We call these "performance ratios." Many owners don't or can't start with these performance ratios, but understand that taking control of the "wage line" for all owners, advisors, and producers through a salary and bonus structure means that, in time, with sustained growth, *things will change*, and improve. All you have to do is plan thoroughly, and take the first step.

Stop the revenue-sharing and/or commission-splitting arrangements and you can grow your way through many of these challenges as you evolve from a practice to a business of enduring value. When 30 percent of your revenues become accessible only to those who actually invest their money and their careers in *your* business, a funny thing will happen: People will start to value ownership and equity. They will want to become equity partners, building on top of what you've built.

PRODUCTION MODEL VERSUS BUSINESS MODEL

So, if building a business with a bottom line makes it more sustainable and more valuable and sets up a strong succession plan, why don't more owners employ this method? The answer lies in the fact that most practice owners tend to focus their efforts almost entirely on production without thinking about the trade-off in terms of equity and enterprise strength. In this section, we compare the production model and the business model works, side-by-side, and show you the math.

A typical arrangement is illustrated in Figure 3.8; assume a fee-based practice with annual gross revenue of $1 million. The producers in this model, including the owner/founder, are paid on a 50 percent revenue-sharing arrangement; in other words, everyone receives 50 percent of every dollar of revenue they produce. After paying the overhead (staff compensation, lease costs, benefits, utilities, marketing, technology, management, etc.), there is little or no meaningful profit.

Most independent practices and businesses operate as pass-through tax conduits (sole proprietorships, S corporations, and LLCs taxed as a

| PRODUCTION MODEL | |
CURRENTLY	
Gross Revenue	$1,000,000
Revenue Share/EWYK	–$500,000
Expenses	–$500,000
Profit	$0

FIGURE 3.8 Typical Production Model

PRODUCTION MODEL	
+5 YEARS (APPROX. 7% GROWTH)	
Gross Revenue	$1,400,000
Revenue Share/EWYK	−$700,000
Expenses	−$700,000
Profit	$0

FIGURE 3.9   Creating a Bottom Line: Current Production Model

disregarded entity, partnership, or S corporation), so actual owners may not consider lack of profits an issue. If the goal is simply to generate a good living and to have maximum individual control over the engine of production, there is nothing wrong with this approach. But consider what this same model looks like five years later (Figure 3.9) when there is little or no meaningful profit compared to the business model in Figure 3.10.

Assuming a 7 percent annual top-line growth rate for the five-year period, the production model has grown at the same rate as the business model. Both have the same top-line revenue, and both owners make about the same amount of money. So what's the difference? Equity. The business model is worth in the neighborhood of $3 million; the production model is unsalable as a business because the nonowners control their own books and it is highly unlikely that all producers will sell in unison. In fairness, the production model is built for producer enrichment, not owner's equity—but with the business model, you have the same production *and* the advantage of equity value.

In the business model, the function of controlling and gradually flattening the compensation line with a salary/bonus structure, as we illustrated in the preceding section, results in a bottom line. The profits, in turn, are reserved for those who legally own and who financially invest in the business—advisors who buy stock from the founder. Because the business model now has two or more owners who focus on the bottom line (and for good reason

BUSINESS MODEL	
+5 YEARS (APPROX. 7% GROWTH)	
Gross Revenue	$1,400,000
Salary/Bonus	−$500,000
Expenses	−$650,000
Profit	$250,000

FIGURE 3.10   Creating a Bottom Line: Business Model in Five Years

since it impacts their take-home pay), expenses tend to be better controlled as well. The margin between revenue growth and expense growth tends to improve, and that further improves the bottom line over time.

The profits generated in the business model are distributed approximately quarterly to the owners in the business. If minority owners want to increase their profit distributions, they will have to think like an owner: (1) grow the top-line revenue (production is still job number one), (2) reduce overhead costs, and/or (3) buy more stock. All of a sudden, the implicit value of ownership has increased without lessening the business's rate of growth. Granted, the compensation systems we examine a thousand times a year are more varied and a little more elaborate than we're illustrating here, but the common denominators in almost every case are some type of EWYK system and a one-owner practice model focused almost exclusively on production.

In sum, remodeling your cash flows means that things are going to be different. You will have to learn to use your financial data more effectively, and that function will make you a better owner and advisor, especially to your business clients. Once these systems and processes are in place, however, most owners find that the cash flow structure is not more complicated—it is more sophisticated. It will increase business formalities, which is to be expected as a business becomes investor-worthy. From the founder's perspective, flexibility (in terms of his/her personal salary and distributions) is gradually exchanged for predictability and reliability, even longevity.

CHAPTER 4

Creating Your Succession Team

THE PEOPLE PROBLEM

So by now, at least figuratively speaking, you've set up the correct entity structure, and you have an organizational structure and a modern compensation system designed to support an enduring and transferable business. But you're still the sole owner (or perhaps one of several owners without a clear plan). Having built the foundation for a successful succession plan, how do you convince the next generation to get on board (as business owners and investors in one, single business) your ship?

Let's just ask it out loud: Will the next generation invest in what you've built? Does it make more sense for them to hang out their own shingle or to build on top of what you've spent the past 10, 20, or 30 years building and growing? These are good, tough questions; let's make them harder, and more relevant: Why would a producer who makes $250,000 a year or more, who has no or minimal responsibilities for hiring, firing, signing leases, negotiating leasehold improvements, or worrying about payroll, want to become an investor, a minority owner in your business? Those are the issues that we're going to focus on in this chapter.

So, what are the answers? Well, for starters, understand that you can offer a very unique investment opportunity, and you will need to learn to articulate it once your plans are complete. Think of it this way: How many investments can a younger advisor make that come with a mentor and a paycheck, and pay for themselves over time? How many active investments start out with the goal of not impacting the investor's take-home pay and provide the investor with the means of giving himself or herself an automatic raise by helping the business grow? A good succession plan will do all of these things.

Remember those first couple of years of self-employment as an independent advisor and the size of the paycheck you received, even after some very long and trying days? You have the ability now, with experience, to help others avoid that pitfall, and that's worth something (it's worth a lot, actually). And that is just one of the reasons that the ownership circle is a special place; not everyone gains admittance.

To build an enduring business, you need more than one owner; it takes people, good people, which is why this may very well be the hardest part of the process. It is impossible to perpetuate a small business without the help and support of next-generation talent. That much is obvious. The more challenging aspects are often summed up in these basic, but often asked questions:

- How do I hire and retain employees with an entrepreneurial mind-set?
- How do I sell or gradually transfer the business to employees who have no extra money to invest?
- What if my internal ownership plan doesn't work out?

Many founding owners struggle with these issues, but the real concern may be better stated as: "How do I find people who will work as hard and care as much about this business as I do?" Too often, however, that question is framed to generate a nearly impossible answer in support of a self-fulfilling prophecy. As the founder, there is only one of you; there will never be another. You're the entrepreneur, and the only one your business will ever need. Entrepreneurs have to do it all in the early years of building a practice, but that process is usually augmented by having a very short and efficient chain of command. The next generation must work collaboratively, as a team, to accomplish its goals—not an easier or a harder task, but very different from what most entrepreneurs in this industry have to do. Regardless, if you don't find a way to share what you've spent a lifetime learning, your practice and your knowledge will die with you.

The better and more exciting news may be this: Creating and supporting an internal ownership track, one designed to support the most common "Lifestyle Succession Plans," as we call them, isn't about replacing you as the founder. Rather, the process is about taking the best of your talents and experiences and using them to build a business of enduring value, something that can outlive you and serve your trusting clients for generations to come. With that goal in mind, let's start with the basics and solve the people problem: Where do you find the talent to form your succession team?

THE SECRET FORMULA: G-1 + G-2 + G-3

One of the consistent points in this book is that independent owners need modern and appropriate tools to work with to build multigenerational businesses— not the tools they've learned to use from the wirehouse side of the industry.

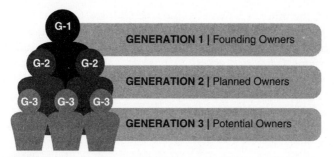

FIGURE 4.1 Building a Multi-Generational Business

To this end, we'd like to introduce some terminology to help you navigate through the people problem. We label these terms "G-1," "G-2," and "G-3." (See Figure 4.1.)

Every succession plan is designed around the unique goals of the founder, whom we call G-1, for Generation One. In the case where there are multiple owners and founders within five years of each other's ages, they are all G-1s. Referencing Figure 4.1 as a general illustration, you'll need to create a succession team, a group of younger owners—all equity partners who buy their way in to the ownership circle, often one at a time. Let's start with Generation Two, or G-2.

Ideally, you're looking for two people at the G-2 level for every owner at the G-1 level, and three people at the G-3 level for every owner at the G-1 level. The perfect age difference between G-1 and G-2 is about 15 years (plus or minus five years); it does not require a family generation, though we frequently see that fact pattern as well. If there are two or more senior owners within five years of each other's age, their average age is the reference point to use when looking for the G-2 personnel for your succession team. It is not necessary that you start your plan with two G-2 advisors right out of the gate for every G-1 level owner; you can solve this problem over the course of the first five years of the plan, but it is important to eventually diversify your risk with a minimum of two G-2 level prospects. In the event that the G-2s are much younger than the ideal, defer to their capabilities and potential rather than age. To paraphrase the late President Reagan, don't hold their youth and inexperience against them.

Why is it important to widen the ownership base? There are three answers to that question that are equally relevant:

1. *Continuity planning.* If, five years into the plan, G-1 has to buy out G-2 because G-2 had a skiing accident or a car accident or quits, the succession plan will shift into dead reverse. G-2 needs a continuity plan that

relies on the other G-2 owner(s), not the founder (G-1), who has a gradual retirement in mind and is in the process of selling off his or her ownership gradually over the next 10 to 20 years to the succession team.

2. *Diversifying G-1's risk.* Many G-1s think that the biggest problem to solve is where G-2 will get the money to buy them out. That is incorrect. The problem is one of tenure. In other words, how do you get a 20- or 30-year-old to make a career-length investment? The fact is, they may not stick with it. Having more than one G-2 owner not only diversifies the risk that one advisor may leave, but it also creates some friendly competition and ensures that the best talent is available to the clients and to lead the business in the years to come.

3. *Diversifying G-2's and G-3's risk.* Buying out G-1's position by paying, in many cases, seven figures of value with after-tax dollars, and trying to track down a business that is growing and accelerating away from the internal buyers, who often have no significant cash reserves at their disposal, is a tall order. Dividing that task among a group of collaborative investors is smart work and smart investing.

Let's stop here and clarify some important points. Most succession plans do not include the sale of the entire practice all at once to a single younger advisor. That scenario is possible, and we've helped advisors successfully do it, but that is more of an exit strategy or an outright sale, not a succession plan. A succession plan is designed to build a multigenerational business by gradually transferring ownership and leadership to a team of next-generation advisors.

G-2 advisors, the most senior members of your succession team, are almost always producers or, if you don't like that term, independent owners who are capable of generating revenue for the business by providing advice and services or selling product. Prospective owners who are a part of a fee-only business (Registered Investment Advisers [RIAs]) don't need to be licensed or able to produce revenue, but they usually are since that is a primary source of their funding to buy your ownership interests, or stock; if you're Financial Industry Regulatory Authority (FINRA) regulated, we recommend restricting the succession team to those who are properly and similarly licensed. For those who are with an independent broker-dealer or insurance company that has unlicensed key staff members, the use of a phantom stock plan may be the better choice for those particular staff members.

If the plan unfolds successfully, it should be G-2's responsibility to hire, train, and retain the G-3 level succession team, with guidance from G-1 of course. The G-3 level owners will be the future business partners for G-2, so let them make some of these decisions, right or wrong. It is part of the learning process for the next generation of business owners, and it is how most G-1s learned how to hire the best people at the G-2 level to succeed them.

Many owners ask us when G-2 should become eligible for an ownership opportunity. How long does a G-2 prospect need to work for you before becoming an equity partner? Our experience is that the time frame in this industry needs to be shorter, at least at this time, than in most other professional service industries where five-plus years is the norm. Advisors are starting late and are in an industry that still encourages separate book building; until that culture significantly changes, plan on working a little harder, and faster, to keep and propel great talent that you have on board or that comes your way. We think that ownership opportunities should be extended to G-2 in years 3 through 5 of full-time employment. For G-3, the partnership track should be extended a bit, probably to around four to six years of full-time employment before a partnership buy-in opportunity is extended.

If you have the opportunity to pick up a great prospect who has just graduated from Texas Tech University or a similar four-year program with a bachelor of science in personal financial planning and at a reasonable cost, do it. Developing a G-3 prospect or two is smart, if you can afford it, but do it as a part of a formal plan. Put them on a W-2 compensation system, share with them your plans for building an enduring business, and see how it goes. It's okay to plug in the talent at all levels and at various intervals. It isn't about the timing; it's about the quality of the people you surround yourself with, and the sooner you do that, the better.

PLAN BEFORE YOU BUILD AND HIRE

When I was in my thirties and had a lot more energy, I used to run long distances, for fun and relaxation. On a Saturday morning, I would routinely run 10 miles or more. On one occasion, I was deep in thought as I ran, mile after mile, and I got lost. (In the days before cell phones, it was a lot easier to do!) Being a little tired and disoriented, I quickly decided to choose the most logical direction and keep on running because it felt good to make progress. But a few miles later, I realized I wasn't making progress by continuing to run in a wrong direction—I was just making the problem worse and slowly running out of energy and daylight. It was time to stop, reassess the situation, and maybe walk for a bit until the path became clearer, which it did.

One of the common refrains we hear from advisors is this: "I don't have anyone who works for me who is ownership material. I've hired a number of people over the years, and most end up being competitors." That shouldn't come as a surprise, in that most likely you didn't hire or train any of these folks to be part of your succession team, let alone to build an enduring business. Hiring a producer/advisor who could become the future CEO of your business, at twice its current size, isn't a matter of luck. Still, regardless of your current talent situation, or maybe in spite of it, you should restart the process with a formal, written plan that lays out what talent you're going to need, and when you're likely to need it. A sample succession plan schematic is provided in Figure 4.2.

For many advisors, typically those around age 50 or more and who also find themselves in business-building mode, succession planning often ends up being the cornerstone of a strategic growth strategy designed to perpetuate the business and the income streams beyond the founder's lifetime. It is the succession planning process, interestingly enough, that is used to assess and fix the structural issues necessary to retain or onboard the necessary next-generation talent.

The real starting point in the business building process requires a focus on two primary areas of work that ideally begin at least another five to 10 years before the succession plan is even launched (think closer to age 40), if not when the practice is initially set up. The two broad-based areas to plan and build around are these:

1. Organizational structuring, which includes creating an equity-centric organization, making your entity investor-friendly, and setting up a professional compensation system for those at the ownership level.
2. Optimizing business resources, which is designed to produce strong, sustainable growth; this is about the people it takes to run a multigenerational business—how to attract them, reward them, and keep them on board for a lifetime.

These items have to be attended to before a formal, written succession plan can be launched (note the far left, gray box in Figure 4.2), but the benefit of implementing these steps goes far beyond the issues surrounding a founding owner's gradual retirement. These are powerful business-building steps, and it is never too soon to start doing things right. The limitations on today's first generation of retiring owners are similar to those on typical advisory clients who first start planning for retirement five to 10 years before they want to start enjoying all the benefits of a lifetime of work and savings. That's not much time to plan with, and even with a great plan, the results have a self-imposed ceiling because of the limited time frame.

The goal of most succession plans is to make the business work for you, instead of the other way around. One of the most important steps in the process of building an enduring and transferable business is to build an investor-worthy enterprise designed from the outset to attract, retain, and empower next-generation talent. Building the foundation should start at

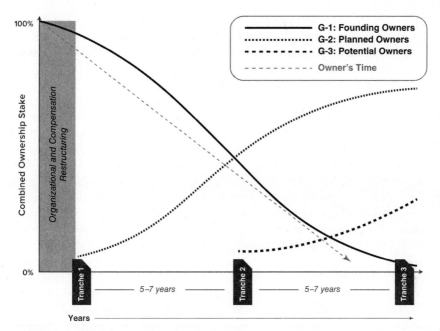

FIGURE 4.2   Succession Planning Schematic

around age 40 for the founder, or when the founding team is, on average, around age 40; this gives you an extra 10 years, or more, to solve many of these problems and, more or less, makes succession planning an easy problem to solve. It shifts the problem from building to where it belongs: planning for the future. Build the foundations for success 10 years earlier than you intend to start your succession planning.

MINING THE TALENT POOL

The result of building the correct foundations for a valuable and enduring business and laying out a formal, written succession plan is that you will be able to offer a unique employment and career opportunity to the next generation of independent professionals. First, you'll be able to offer an ownership opportunity with a built-in financing structure. Second, you will be able to offer not only a competitive wage, but also access to your company's substantial future profit distributions for all partners. Finally, you'll be able to offer them control over their future and an enhanced income stream (wages + profits + equity), with the added protection of a collaborative framework that ensures a sound continuity plan and succession plan.

That is a powerful package, but what happens if the next-generation talent isn't buying what you're selling? The norm in this industry, right or wrong, is an activity-based compensation package that rewards production. What about those advisors who refuse to work for anything other than a share of revenue or an eat-what-you-kill approach? The best answer is this: Go back to your plan and revisit the fundamentals and the goals. It is important that you understand how the pieces are linked together to create a strong framework for long-term success, to transform your practice into an enduring business. Then be prepared to explain it patiently and confidently.

When you share revenues, you exchange cash flow for equity. You receive, after expenses, the smaller share of the cash flow that has been produced, and you give away all of the equity value of the book (only to turn around and buy it back if the advisor later decides to come on board as an owner). If a revenue-sharing arrangement is what they really want, and they won't listen to your point of view, may I suggest you send them down the street to your nearest competitor and let them take the equity out of someone else's practice? Unless you are trying to build a wirehouse of your own, you don't benefit from a revenue-sharing arrangement as a business builder.

Over the past five years, we've had the very special opportunity to sit and privately talk to second- and third-generation advisors, G-2 and G-3 respectively, and to show them the plans we've come up with for G-1, the founder of the company. We explain how we valued the business they are being offered an ownership opportunity in, and how they can use this tool to track the annual value of their investment. We explain the upside and the downside of the investment opportunity, all without G-1 in the room.

We explain that the investment doesn't start with a pay cut (their current take-home pay isn't typically needed for the buy-in process), and that the success of the investment will require that they invest more than their money. The investments we're looking for are tied to the strengths they bring to the table: their time, their energy, and their careers.

We show them the pro forma spreadsheet and what's in it for them and what's in it for their boss and the other members of the succession team that will need to be hired, trained, and who may earn and be offered a similar opportunity. We show them that by producing, and by growing the company, they control, to a large extent, their own means of compensation and paying off the obligations of purchasing equity and building wealth for themselves. We show them what we hope the future of their investment will look like—the nature of a pro forma—if they do their job as a collaborative, long-term business partner.

And then it gets more exciting. We invite them to return for a second call with their spouses, or significant others, or coaches, or whomever they turn to for advice when making big decisions. And we do it all over again. We do this with hundreds of G-2 and G-3 advisors every year, and 85 percent of them decide to invest and commit their careers or at least 10 years at a time to the process of building on top of an existing business, to build something as a team. They sign a stock purchase agreement and a promissory note, and they buy stock (or ownership interest in an LLC) from G-1. They agree to flatten their compensation at the wage level, and they turn to a share of profit distributions for their pay increases. Are they really ready for this? They think so!

In our conversations with founders of businesses in this industry years after implementing a succession plan and setting up the foundational structures, we hear them use terms like "rejuvenated" and "reenergized." We see it in their growth rates. We hear it in their voices. Most G-1 level owners tell us that they're beginning to work less hard, they're doing more of the things they enjoy, and they think their careers will actually be extended, allowing them to contribute more and to really make a difference, while still throttling back on work hours and stress. These are the common goals of most succession plans.

TURNING EMPLOYEES INTO EQUITY PARTNERS

The first place to look for your succession team talent is internally—the people who work for you now. While these folks probably weren't hired or recruited with ownership and succession planning in mind, they still deserve to be considered and auditioned for this important opportunity, if it is done properly and as part of a well-structured plan. There are basically two kinds of internal staff members that can support the goals of a succession plan:

1. Key employees/advisors without their own books
2. Key employees/advisors with their own books

For the most part, when we refer to key employees or staff members, we mean that they are active participants who produce revenue and are therefore licensed, registered, or qualified to provide investment advice or sell various products or services. Fee-only RIAs have more latitude in this area, whereas FINRA-regulated advisors have less; either way, plans can usually be tailored to fit the circumstances.

Key staff members who do not have their own books tend to be paid on a W-2 basis (think salary and bonus), but form of payment is not material as the plan is initially designed and developed. Simply stated, consider the best staff members for an ownership opportunity almost regardless of age. Determine where an existing employee (or even a potential new hire) fits into your plan, or might fit with further growth and development. In doing so, picture your business at twice its current size (i.e., twice the cash flow, but understanding that doubling everything, including workload and expenses and number of clients, likely won't be how you double in value). In that setting, where will you need additional help, what roles will you need to fill, how many hours will you want to be working at that time, and where will talent be needed to strengthen the business model?

It is a common mistake to conclude that a given employee isn't an entrepreneur like the founder of the business, especially when the employee doesn't have his or her own book. But honestly, doesn't every successful advisor start from zero at some point in his or her career? The issue is that the founders often look for younger versions of themselves—an obvious chance to repeat a process that worked so well the first time. It bears repeating that building on top of an existing business is going to require a very different skill set than starting a business from scratch. An established business can present a truly unique investment opportunity for succeeding generations of advisors that does not require one person to do it all. It will take more than one person to run a great business.

Start slowly and slot your key staff member(s) in at G-2 or G-3 in your plan, and offer them an ownership opportunity. Plan on selling around 5 percent to 7.5 percent at most to each individual in this first round, and offer them 10-year seller financing. Do not give away ownership; it should be sold and purchased—this is part of the proving grounds. Remember, there are two sides to this investment opportunity, and while G-1 typically retains the roles of CEO and president, and is the majority owner at this point in the plan, the next generation has a decision to make, too. Don't take the decision on whether to become an owner and invest a career out of their hands with a gift of ownership; both sides of this equation need to evaluate it on the merits and make the hard decision. Clearing this hurdle is often part of the process of valuing the opportunity and making it work. Strategic grants of stock can and often are still a part of the overall strategy, just not right out of the gate.

Are there hooks in this ownership opportunity? Absolutely; in fact, there's a net over this ownership opportunity. Every next-generation purchase of stock (or ownership interest) is secured with a stock pledge, a restrictive continuity agreement, drag-along rights, penalties for not finishing the process, and so on. That said, don't forget to plan adequately for success and to provide incentives for achieving your mutual goals. Many first-time purchases of ownership include friendly financing that is almost default-proof, and additional, small grants of stock over time (only after stock is first purchased and paid for), and sometimes a minority discount. All in all, it's a pretty good deal.

FP Transitions' Lifestyle Succession Plan relies on a multiple-tranche strategy that can be adjusted to create a long-term, flexible approach that results in a very gradual but significant reduction of the G-1 level advisor's time spent in the business as the reins of leadership are earned and handed off. The process begins with the acquisition of stock by the G-2 level advisor(s) on a tranche basis (the number of tranches or steps are designed to fit the circumstances of the business and its owners, but two to five tranches are the norm for planning purposes) from G-1's perspective. Appropriately, Tranche 1 is often called the incubator. It is designed to test whether the next-generation advisors you have on staff, or those you add to your staff, value this opportunity and investment as much as you do.

Tranche 2 may never happen, and it will happen only if the G-2 level owners prove themselves worthy in Tranche 1. If your plan doesn't work out (and that's a possibility), plan B is to position what you've built for sale or merger. Before you get to that point, recognize that setting up and administering an internal ownership track takes time, and sometimes you have to restart the process. The more time you give yourself, the more likely it is that you'll get it right and create an excellent succession plan.

ONBOARDING TALENT WITH A BOOK OF BUSINESS

As for the second group, key staff members who have their own books, this can be a bit more treacherous, but often has much greater upside. This group is the most likely to form your G-2 contingent. It almost doesn't matter whether the producer/advisor works for you directly as an employee, works under your roof as a contractor, or is a new or prospective recruit; onboarding an individual with his or her own book into an ownership slot in your growing business is a challenging but potentially lucrative maneuver. Understand that bringing this group into the owners' circle will take a higher level of skill than the previous group and requires a better understanding of how the structural elements in your business work together to make it possible, and advantageous for both sides.

Advisors in this class are a proven commodity, at least in one respect. They can generate revenue. That does not and should not automatically qualify them for ownership, but it is a major consideration. The bigger questions that naturally follow are: Do they want to sacrifice the control they enjoy over their workdays and income stream in exchange for a minority ownership position, some significant debt, and the opportunity to build on top of your business? Can they do anything more than produce revenue? Are they a good fit with the rest of the team? Those can be tough questions to answer, but they are impossible to answer if you don't have a plan for what you're trying to build and that clearly illustrates the benefits for all involved.

We see three common scenarios when onboarding advisor/producers with their own books into an equity position:

1. The book is small enough and the employer/employee relationship strong enough to make the issue irrelevant.
2. The book is large enough and valuable enough that G-1 buys it with an exchange of ownership or very advantageous financing.
3. The book is large enough and the advisor capable enough that he or she walks across the street and hangs out his or her own shingle, or legitimately threatens to rather than build on top of your business ("The Case of the Super Producer" is covered in the following section).

If you helped G-2 get started with knowledge and/or a contribution of your smaller clients, and if you don't wait too long, and if the value and cash flow from the book is not too great (typically not more than about $150,000 in gross revenue, or GDC), it often isn't difficult to onboard this talent level into an ownership position. Assuming that your plan provides the basic elements of seller financing at discounted levels and a profit-based note (at least in the first tranche), you have an excellent chance of making this level of advisor an equity partner. Granted, that is a pretty good list of "ifs," but it is far better to try to build a collaborative, long-term relationship than watch yet another advisor/producer grow stronger and become your competitor. Develop a plan and give it a try, and don't offer too many concessions; all in all, the opportunity is a good one for the next-generation advisor and he or she is in the business of taking advantage of good investments. Show the advisor your plan for the future and where they fit in. Remember, equity is a powerful draw, and you'll see that in the pro forma models for your long-term plan—so will G-2.

In short order, here's how it tends to work. The onboarding process starts with an evaluation period—with due diligence being performed in both directions. Remember the general timeframes from earlier—extend an ownership opportunity to G-2 in years 3 through 5 of full-time employment. For G-3, the partnership track should be extended a bit, probably around four to six years of full-time employment before a partnership buy-in opportunity is extended. Don't keep your plans a secret—in fact, share your plans from the first interview on, and then see how it goes.

When the time comes to seriously consider an ownership opportunity, start by having your business and the advisor/producer's practice formally valued (but only if their book is larger than about $150,000 in gross revenue or GDC), and then have two copies of the valuation results made and certified; share one complete copy with the other side (be sure to sign a nondisclosure agreement beforehand, and use a common valuation methodology). Share a copy of your comprehensive succession plan with your onboarding prospect and explain what you're thinking, where the prospect fits in, and what's in this for both of you.

If interest remains strong and it is a good match after additional thought and exploration, you'll need to physically bring the two models together to operate side by side and under the same roof (if they aren't already). This is not a merger or a marriage, just two owners moving in together to see if a permanent union is warranted and wise. This might sound quaint or old-fashioned, but this is a big step, and creating a permanent equity partner out of a satellite office with someone you only talk to over the phone is often impractical and unworkable, at least if your goal is to build one strong enduring business.

If it works out, the owner of the book, the prospective G-2 producer/advisor, will sign a contribution agreement and contribute all right, title, and interest in the book to your business. Your business, in exchange, can use its treasury stock (authorized but unissued shares) to purchase the book, often using the respective values of the business and the book to determine the correct ownership ratio, or at least to form the starting point for the negotiations. On this point, G-1 often argues that G-2 has no infrastructure and no "real business," and that somehow that mitigates or even eliminates any value to the G-2 book. That is a good argument, but it almost always loses. The simple retort is that G-2 won't do that deal and sacrifice autonomy and control over his or her cash flow for an at-will employment situation and a minority ownership position and a formal debt obligation, and why would they?

The bigger issue is taxes. If you are set up or taxed as an S corporation, the owner of the book of business who exchanges what that advisor/producer has built for an ownership position in your business is taxed on the fair market value of the stock received just as if he or she had sold the book and been paid for it (from the IRS's perspective, that is exactly what happens). That's a nonstarter for G-2 unless the transaction also includes a significant cash payment, which tends to make it a nonstarter for G-1 as well. The more common solution for this problem goes back to the element of long-term, friendly financing and the ability to buy in on a discounted basis with profit distributions largely derived from the future growth of the business; the after-tax effects are mitigated by time and cash flow mechanisms.

In other words, a smaller book serves more as the "ticket onto your ship" than an immediate windfall and automatic and full equity position.

The process might sound complicated, but we've seen it done hundreds and hundreds of times—it works, if you know what you're doing. The equity position will be immediate, but the equity is usually bought and paid for on an installment basis over time using future growth and profit distributions to make the payments and sometimes the process will need to be augmented with stock grants. Experience dictates that most G-2's/G-3's will take this deal and run.

The S corporation entity structure is rigid and inflexible which correlates to a rather predictable result given the limited but straight-forward options available. That can be a very good thing. The LLC model, in contrast, at least when taxed as a partnership can offer some distinct tax advantages and flexibility when faced with these issues, so if onboarding talent is a possibility, the LLC structure is probably the better entity choice. Regardless, the problem is solvable if both sides see the advantages of working together and want to solve the problem. Taxes are always a high hurdle, but almost never an impenetrable wall.

THE CASE OF THE SUPER PRODUCER

If the book is large enough that it becomes a negotiating point, life is about to become more interesting. Not to belabor the issue, but this is exactly why you should stop using revenue-sharing arrangements and building in those fracture lines that you'll later have to work to overcome and pay to weld back together. It is possible to onboard these larger books, and our success rates seem to be around 50/50, but the process is more complicated in terms of legalities and tax repercussions and ownership-level compensation and the situation can reach a point where it can no longer be recovered or saved. This is the case of the super producer.

There is no magic number to define a "super producer," but start by thinking about revenue streams upwards of $250,000 (i.e., the amount of money that the producer takes home from their share of the eat-what-you-kill or revenue-sharing compensation system. It is not unusual to see super producers taking home upwards of $500,000 to $1,000,000 per year, and the process becomes more challenging the higher the level of production. Super producers often are very experienced, very confident, and they are well rewarded for focusing on and excelling at really just one thing—making it rain.

Super producers often find themselves in an interesting position. They get paid as much or more than most owners. They control their own work day, they have few of the headaches that owners have (payroll, hiring, firing, training administrative staff members, signing an office lease, executing a line of credit, etc.), and they take on very little risk in terms of building a business and creating or investing in infrastructure. But super producers, as we're defining the term, are not shareholders. They have no equity stake in the business under whose roof they work. They are often treated like a partner, and often called a partner, but they are not. Super producers don't get paid last like an equity partner does—they get paid first, right off the top line.

Super producers commonly argue that, while not an equity partner of the overall business, they are indeed an owner—they own "something." On this point, they're right. They have control over cash flow and client relationships and that can translate into real value and real equity. Most super producers don't reach that level of production on their own and without ongoing support, so the question often shifts to "Is the book sustainable if taken to the street?" Interestingly, this tends to remain largely a theoretical issue as the book and its owner aren't interested in setting up a stand-alone, fully competitive business model, though it may take time for this realization to emerge. At the same time, they're not typically excited about becoming a minority owner and an at-will employee of a larger business.

The negotiation pattern often includes a certain level of brinksmanship, but more often than not, these models are successfully onboarded one way or another, at one time or another. Super producers have a lot of control over cash flow, with the understanding that they rely on someone else's infrastructure investment to survive and prosper. Regardless of the bravado and confidence that comes with high levels of production and low levels of risk, super producers have a significant weakness—their cash flow is nearly worthless if they ever stop working, die, or become disabled. G-1 can exert a significant amount of influence over that book and the client relationships that generate the cash flow in G-2's absence (i.e., in the event of G-2's death or disability) and as a result, the book is often not saleable or transferable without G-1's agreement. The older a super producer gets, the clearer this issue becomes. In the end, super producers and the businesses that they are affiliated with are usually better off together than separate and that is what both sides eventually figure out, though with a fair amount of hand-wringing and angst along the way.

The onboarding process typically follows the pattern outlined in the previous section, and again yields to the realities of the entity structure and taxes. The super producer contributes all right, title and interest in his/her book in exchange for a buy-in opportunity that has a few more incentives added in (at least when compared to a smaller book). The major difference is not in how the equity is acquired, but rather in how much equity is acquired—super producers have a first-class ticket onto your ship, not a coach-class ticket.

In the end, even if an equity position for the super producer does not work out, there is a tolerable fallback position. Think back to the life raft and ship parable. It is possible to coexist as two different models. If you and the prospective G-2 candidate can't get the deal done, it does not mean that the relationship has to end. Cash flow is still a valuable commodity in a growing business, and circumstances might be better years from now to warrant revisiting the issue. In the meantime, allow the life raft (G-2) to tie up alongside your ship (G-1) and enjoy the benefits of the continuing revenue-sharing arrangement. You have the benefits of the advisor/producer's knowledge, camaraderie, and cash flow; he or she gets to enjoy the benefits and infrastructure of a larger business and the protection it can provide (think continuity arrangement), while earning a good living and retaining 100 percent of his or her own equity value. It can work, and often does.

As in the previous section, being organized as an LLC and taxed as a partnership can provide a lot of flexibility and some important options and tools for solving the case of the super producer.

HELP WANTED AD

If you're looking for a G-2 or G-3 level advisor, you may well need to mine the talent pool and run a help wanted ad. Businesses require good people who are willing to work hard and make long-term commitments. Finding the right people and subsequently retaining them often starts with the right hiring process.

This is hard work and it is an imperfect process that requires careful decisions and a quick trigger if (maybe *when* is the better word) you're wrong. Better to restart the process than labor to make a poor fit seem like a good fit. My G-1 partner, Brad, has a great saying on the hiring process: "When expectations turn into hopes, it's over."

From our perspective, the best source of great people is a referral from a trusted source. Still, cast the net wide and interview as many qualified people as you can find. But don't hire someone and try to find a plan the person fits into; set up a clear, long-range succession plan first and hire the people you will need to achieve your professional and financial goals. In general, as a growing business, hire for a business twice your size and plan accordingly. Hiring without understanding your end-game strategy often turns into a disaster—or worse, in this industry, a group of separate books that turn into competitors.

Consider placing an ad or notice like this in a number of locations, including online sources (don't forget your own website by including a tab for "Career Opportunities"), your local Financial Planning Association (FPA) chapter, your local AICPA chapter, and with the local colleges, depending on the talent and age level you're searching for:

Seeking an Experienced Financial Advisor

ABC Financial Services, LLC is an established financial advisory firm serving clientele in the southwestern United States from our main office in Scottsdale, Arizona. We are in the family wealth management business focusing on high net worth individuals, families, and business owners. Through a planning process built on integrity, knowledge, and attention to every last detail, we seek to guide and inform our clients to successfully navigate the various phases of financial and wealth management. We have been serving this area and market niche for over 25 years and we have a constantly evolving succession plan in place to ensure that we'll be here 50 years from now.

This is a special opportunity unlike most in the financial services industry. First, our firm is completely independent, so our loyalty belongs exclusively to our clients. Second, we offer a competitive compensation structure (salary and a bonus) and an equity ownership track for employees who demonstrate hard work and leadership characteristics and support the long-term goals of our firm. You will be a member of a collaborative and supportive team of strong individuals, all working hard to help us grow a successful and multigenerational business. At ABC Financial, you won't "own a job" or be building your own practice; this is not an eat-what-you-kill position, and we're not that kind of a firm.

If you are a financial advisor with [#] or more years of experience and an established client base, we encourage you to contact us and explore an opportunity with our firm. All inquiries will be held in strict confidence. At a minimum, candidates should be able to bring the following assets to the firm:

- *[$] assets under management*
- *[#] years of experience working with high net worth individuals/ families and business owners*
- *Awareness of financial planning issues related to managing wealth*
- *Bachelor's degree and Series 65/66 or CFP designation*
- *Familiarity with portfolio management, including tactical asset allocation, traditional and nontraditional asset classes, and various*

investing styles is a minimum requirement. We prefer sophisticated estate planning, tax planning, education planning, and insurance planning knowledge, as well as strong knowledge of the stock market and macroeconomic trends

- *Attention to detail; strong organizational skills; ability to complete work in a timely, accurate, and thorough manner*
- *Must be personable and punctual, and a problem solver*
- *Clean disciplinary record*

Advisors who meet the above criteria may inquire confidentially about this opportunity by submitting a cover letter and resume to [HR Manager] at _____.

SOLVING THE TALENT CRISIS IN THIS INDUSTRY

Depending on the publication and the writer, the average age of an independent financial professional or advisor seems to range from 50 to 60 years of age. Based on our past 1,000 completed valuation clients, the average age of an owner is 52. Based on our observations as we stand in front of groups of advisors 100 times a year, there is a lot of gray hair in the audience. Since older often means wiser, that's not necessarily a bad thing, until older translates into the attrition model because there are no internal, next-generation advisors to take over. The bottom line is that this industry is getting older, and the complaints about lack of next-generation talent are growing louder.

Still, it is our opinion that the aging of the independent financial services industry is but a symptom of a bigger problem. This profession no more has a problem with aging than a reservoir with a bad leak suffers from a lack of new water supplies.

The problem this industry faces is not a lack of new, younger, and qualified advisor talent; it is a lack of talent willing to work their way up a ladder that is nothing more than a mirage. It isn't that younger, next-generation talent can't see the opportunities in this industry—it's just the opposite. They see what's going on very clearly, and they pass up the opportunity to build a one-generational, valuable practice that is totally dependent on one individual selling products, services, or advice. In some ways, they should be commended for smart thinking and stellar observational skills and running away from this opportunity toward another that is better and more lucrative and rewarding. It is not their job to fix this industry—it is ours.

When younger advisors or prospective financial professionals are successfully recruited into a practice that has no future beyond the career or life of its founder and that founder is in the last 10 years of his or her career, the natural tendency is for new recruits to build their own practices or books; there is no better choice. Said another way, if there is no enduring business to invest in, each next generation of advisors starts to build their own practices and we're caught in a perpetual loop. Older practices die off and new practices spring up on a continual basis, but using the same assembly tools and compensation methods, the results are equally predictable. That is not an attractive proposition to anyone other than a professional recruiter.

Solving the talent crisis in this industry is well within reach. Think about it. Independent financial practices and businesses provide an excellent living often tied to recurring or predictable revenue, earned at relatively low cost, with the highest equity value of any professional services model. What's not to like? The short answer is the lack of enduring business models that enable this industry to more rapidly evolve, improve, and recruit the best of the next-generation talent base. This industry should be the leader in planning and building professional service models, and one day, we think it will be.

A CONVERSATION WITH THE NEXT GENERATION

I recently had the opportunity to present to a group of students from Texas Tech University about the industry they were about to enter into, what to look for in a future employer, and what to avoid. Before getting into the specifics of my conversation with this group of next generation advisors, it is important to acknowledge the work of people like John Gilliam, PhD, CFP, CLU, ChFC, who is an Associate Professor and Director of the Master's Programs at Texas Tech University in the Department of Personal Financial Planning. John's work, and that of many others like him at the university level across this country, is critical to the future of the independent financial services industry and our ability to help advisors build enduring and transferable businesses.

The students we spoke to wanted to know how they could identify a business or a firm that could provide the necessary level of mentoring and one day offer them an ownership opportunity, if they earned it of course. They also wanted to know how they could identify and avoid a practice model that would not survive its founder's retirement, death, or disability.

Our advice to every G-3 advisor prospect we talk to is this: First, concentrate your search on the independent side of the industry where there is a culture of ownership. The wirehouse side, even the insurance side of this industry as it is currently structured, offers an opportunity to make money and to learn, but zero opportunity to become a shareholder or an owner with a real equity position. Those can be good models to learn your craft in, but they are the wrong models if you aspire to ownership or becoming an entrepreneur in your own right.

Second, understand that you may need to separate the learning opportunity from the ownership opportunity, at least in the early years of your career. We tell you this, G-3, so that you can separate an opportunity to learn and earn an income at an independent practice, from an opportunity to accomplish those goals and participate in an ownership track with a business or a firm. In other words, in some circumstances, it isn't enough to want to become an owner—many practices are too small to ever offer the opportunity, but that doesn't mean you can't benefit from working there. There are tens of thousands of small, independent practices that offer an opportunity to learn and grow in a hands-on environment. Just understand what the long-term prospects are going in.

Third, *do not* accept a revenue-sharing arrangement (where you receive a percentage of everything you produce) or any form of an eat-what-you-kill compensation structure. Negotiate for a salary and bonus structure. If you're offered a revenue-sharing arrangement, *run*. That is an operation that will die in the end anyway; it is just a matter of when. If you are in the position of having to sacrifice an ownership opportunity in an enduring business in order to get a job and make some money, don't do further damage by taking on the risk of ownership-like production before you're ready. There are better jobs available.

In terms of how to approach an employer with your desire to become an owner, be honest, and be humble. Tell them that you'll work hard (and understand that my generation does not consider 8 to 5 to be hard work!), and that you'll do what is necessary to succeed within the boundaries provided to you (i.e., recognize that this is a highly regulated industry where initiative is appreciated, as long as you don't go too far), and that you're willing to invest a career, but would like to have an opportunity to buy-in to the firm; say it that way, or they may think you expect to be compensated with ownership. Gauge their reaction and adjust from there. If they react negatively, or they seem put-off, understand that more than 95 percent of the practice and business owners in this industry are one-owner, one-generational models. You can't fix that, so in the end, or at some point early in your career, you're looking for the 4 percent or 5 percent that can offer something more. They're out there.

Here's how to find them. In general, you want a firm with at least 60 percent recurring revenue (fees or trails). You need a firm that is an entity (look for an "Inc." or an "LLC" after their name). You need them to be with an IBD or a custodian. There are more than 4,000 broker-dealers in this country, and you'll have heard of maybe 50. Focus instead on the leader of the business you want to work for. When the opportunity arises, or through your own due diligence, ask and obtain answers to these simple questions:

- Is this business strong and growing?
- Does your business have a succession plan?
- How many owners does this business currently have?
- Do you anticipate this business having more owners in the future?

The independent financial services industry is an excellent career choice. Make the first step into it a good one.

CHAPTER 5

The First Step—A Continuity Plan

A DRESS REHEARSAL FOR SUCCESSION PLANNING

The single biggest threat to an independent practice with one owner or one primary advisor is not the lack of a succession plan; it is the lack of a plan to protect the clients and the owner's cash flow and value in the event of his or her sudden death or disability (temporary or permanent). In the smaller and more common one-owner, one-generational *practice* models, a continuity plan must often look outward for its protection and support and to realize its value, usually from a replacement owner. A properly constructed *business* continuity plan provides for uninterrupted client service and the protection of business value by helping to ensure that the remaining owner(s) has/have the necessary talent, numbers, and funding to continue to run and grow the business while buying out a former owner. In the context of a continuity plan, practices and businesses face very different challenges.

If you've built a multigenerational business or are well on the road to doing so, your continuity plan will derive from your succession plan. An internal ownership track, once implemented and in place, is the best continuity plan available, as clients' needs are addressed by other principals who are invested in the same business; at least in theory, they cannot individually do well unless the business as a whole does well. But that process takes time to design and implement, and, currently, our estimates are that this group comprises only a small fraction of the independent industry. For the vast majority of advisors, it works the other way around: Continuity is the first planning problem to solve because it poses the most immediate and serious threat to a lifetime of work and value and the clients' well-being. For this reason, and for most independent advisors, continuity planning is best thought of as a dress rehearsal for the succession planning process.

This conclusion, and the continuity planning process in general, is also impacted by an advisor's age and career length. As previously noted, most advisors wait until at least age 50 before starting the succession planning process, 20 years or more into their careers. Continuity planning cannot or certainly should not wait that long regardless of the size or structure of your enterprise. Unless you're going to set up a formal succession plan prior to age 50, you need to start the planning process with the continuity aspects front of mind, not with who will be your successor and when and how you'll retire.

Independent financial services practices are among the most valuable professional services models in the United States. But because those same practices are built primarily around the skill set and personality of an individual advisor, that same value proposition is actually quite fragile; within a business with two or more owners, the value proposition is more durable, but not indestructible. Establishing a continuity plan to protect that value, and the client's needs, is one of the most important and challenging aspects of being an independent financial services practice owner.

WHAT EXACTLY IS A CONTINUITY PLAN?

A continuity plan is an emergency plan that assures a seamless transfer of control and responsibility in the event of a sudden departure from the practice or business of any of its owners, young or old, and whether by choice or through termination of employment, or death or disability, or even partnership disputes—okay, not always an emergency, but prompted by something relatively sudden and by things we hope don't happen.

Remember that a succession plan is a professional and written plan designed to build on top of an existing practice or business and to seamlessly and gradually transition ownership and leadership to the next generation. The achievement of these goals, however, assumes that the founder and all the advisors who are part of that plan will live long, healthy, productive lives and that each will remain a part of the same business for the duration; but many times, that just isn't the case. For that reason, every succession plan needs to incorporate a separate continuity or "what if?" plan—in other words, one plan for the long term, one plan for the short term; you need both levels of planning and in a coordinated fashion.

| LEVEL 1 | SUCCESSION PLAN |
| LEVEL 2 | CONTINUITY PLAN |

A continuity plan results in a formal, written continuity agreement. There are many kinds of continuity agreements, and the choice as to which is the best agreement tends to revolve around the number of owners of the practice or business, the type of entity, and what you are attempting to protect against. It further depends on whether the multiple owners own individual books in a practice model or they are shareholders or members of a single business or firm. Even regulatory and compliance issues can significantly impact the choice of plan and continuity partner. Regulators expect that you'll have a business continuity plan that will protect against a significant business disruption such as a natural disaster or power outages. It's advisable that you also protect against death or disability of the business owner(s).

For some financial professionals, especially those in a practice model, the first and only solution is to purchase a life insurance policy, a solution that completely ignores the needs and welfare of the client base and any staff members—a practice not only built to die, but planning on it! The secondary solution is a two- or three-page revenue-sharing agreement that we'll discuss later. Many of the advisors we talk to argue that these approaches are better than nothing, and while that's certainly true, that isn't setting the bar very high. In this chapter, we explain some other and probably better approaches for you to consider.

A continuity plan, even one that takes the form of a written buy-sell agreement or shareholders' agreement or is embedded within an operating agreement, is *not* a succession plan. It can support a succession plan. It can lead to a succession plan, but it is not and never will be a plan for succession—two different things.

BASIC COMPONENTS OF A CONTINUITY PLAN

The most comprehensive and effective continuity agreements are those between shareholders or partners in a single business. These agreements are quite common to business owners and have a variety of titles depending on the circumstances; they may include a shareholders' agreement, a buy-sell agreement, a partnership agreement, or an operating agreement. Using these agreements as the standard-bearers for this category of planning, here is a list of the basic elements that should be addressed in a formal continuity agreement:

- Identify and define the triggering events (death, disability, loss of license, termination of employment, etc.).
- Define what *disability* or *disabled* means and when it triggers the buyout process.

- Provide for an accurate and industry-specific valuation method for determining fair market value of the exiting owner's shares or ownership interest; don't use a multiple of revenue or a basic formula (more on this later).
- Provide for reasonable payment terms, taking into account the possible loss of clients, the need to stabilize and grow the business in the years to come, the need to replace the exiting owner, and the tax impact on the buyer.
- Determine who the buyer will be (the company by redemption, the remaining shareholders on a pro rata basis, a remaining shareholder, or an outside third party) and the order in which they will be selected.
- Provide for the orderly sale of the business (or ownership interest) to a third party in the event no employees or partners elect to step forward.
- Provide for funding through life insurance and lump-sum disability insurance, tying the value of each to the results of a formal valuation as the agreement is executed and regularly thereafter.
- Provide for information to the continuity partner or guardian so that he or she can step in on a moment's notice and operate computers, ensure payroll is met, talk to the staff as well as the clients, and access the client management software.

These agreements are not of the "one and done" variety; they need to be reviewed and updated on a regular basis, especially if the business is growing fast; if ownership changes in any way (people or shares, by purchase, sale, or grant); if the economy changes significantly; or as value increases by more than $100,000 in any given year. It is not necessary to continually buy more insurance to fund these agreements as the business grows; insurance is often an integral part of the funding solution, but rarely the sole means of a buyout.

TYPES OF AGREEMENTS

The type of continuity agreement that is appropriate for your situation depends largely on what you own at the time the agreement is executed. If you own a practice, the common solution is a revenue-sharing agreement. If you own a business, or are in the process of building one, your choices and level of continuity protection are greatly increased.

Revenue-Sharing Agreements

Now, having started with the best continuity planning solution (formal partners in a single, enduring business), let's discuss the most popular solution, recalling that 95 percent of independent financial service professionals are one-owner practices. Continuity planning is especially challenging for the single-owner practice.

The most common continuity solution for a single-owner practice derives from the most commonly used compensation structure—a revenue-sharing arrangement. Independent broker-dealers and custodians routinely hand out short-form contracts (two or three pages in length is typical) to their advisors at no charge, as a substitute for a formal or more comprehensive continuity plan in the event of a disaster. These continuity agreements, often called something like an "Agreement for Assignment of Accounts," allow a seller and a buyer or continuity partner to agree on terms of sale in the event of an advisor's death, permanent disability, or retirement.

Let's be honest. There really is no continuity; there is a replacement advisor within the same broker-dealer or custodial network, who will end up taking over the practice with virtually no risk, and paying only 60 to 70 cents on the dollar, and doing things his/her way almost without regard for what you promised your clients. These are great deals for a buyer—there is nothing to lose. For the seller, these work if you place no significant value on what you've built and don't really need the money that might come from the agreement. For the broker-dealer or custodian, it's the only way to practically (and efficiently) exert any control over the client base and help ensure they stay within the network. Equity is not the issue.

Regardless of the broker-dealer or custodian, the forms are pretty much all the same. Most include provisions such that the advisor who takes over the client accounts or relationships (typically called the "assignee") will pay to the disabled advisor or to the deceased advisor's estate (the "assignor") X percent of the revenues earned for Y years. The assignee is not obligated to make any payments on client accounts not serviced by the assignee, who has the unilateral ability to decide for himself or herself which accounts to service and which ones to let go. There is no down payment to help motivate the assignee to service most of the accounts, or to service them well. Should anything happen to the assignee, or if the assignee changes to a different broker-dealer, the agreement usually contains an immediate termination clause.

The arrangement typically applies only to management fees and insurance renewal commissions, or trails (the sales commission–based portion of the practice is given a value of zero even if there is a historical track record of repeatable and consistent sales commissions), and provides that the designated percentage of those revenue streams be paid out by the broker-dealer or custodian to the retiring advisor or to his or her surviving spouse, estate, or other designated beneficiary. Taxes are commonly ignored, and that usually means that instead of long-term capital gains, the seller receives the proceeds at ordinary income tax rates. Most contain no provisions for settling a dispute or verifying the income received by the buyer.

The truth is that these agreements mirror the way most practices are assembled and built, so it is only natural to use a similar tool to take them apart and bring them to an end. This is part of the cycle of building a practice designed to die from the outset. If that is acceptable to you, and to your broker-dealer or custodian, then use these forms and don't look back.

Here's the bottom line: For a one-owner practice with less than about $200,000 in gross revenue at its peak, revenue-sharing arrangements are the best solution. They're quick, cheap, and capable of delivering about 60 to 70 cents on the dollar, depending on the circumstances and the economy. But for every advisor above that level, and as an industry, we have to do better than this and we can. "Better than nothing" can never be allowed to be the standard for an independent advisor. Would you ever provide that answer to your clients when they inevitably ask the question: "What happens to me if something happens to you?"

A Guardian Agreement

A continuity plan should always address and define triggering events such as death, disability, or termination of employment, but the plan also needs to consider the very real possibility of a temporary change in operating control or the delivery of services. This situation might occur when an advisor is injured in an auto accident and he or she is unable to work for five to six months, but then returns to the practice or business. The guardian agreement was a concept that we first introduced to this industry in 2008, but honestly, we've never been able to make it work effectively for 95 percent or more of this industry.

As designed, a guardian agreement allows another advisor, or guardian, to manage the practice temporarily in the event of an advisor's disability. The guardian is appropriately compensated for the services he or she provides until the disabled advisor is able to return to work, or until the practice can be sold to a third party. On rare occasions, this role is filled by another advisor unaffiliated with the disabled or deceased advisor's practice; sometimes this role is filled by a key employee, son, or daughter, or, more commonly, by a minority shareholder who simply isn't in a position to buy and run the practice permanently or by a larger shareholder who is.

This is a very real problem to solve for, especially for advisors in their 50s, 60s, or 70s, of which there are more than a few. But for one-owner independent practices it is quite difficult to provide any meaningful, compliant, and practical coverage on a temporary basis by an outside party, even another advisor with the same broker-dealer or custodian and operating in the same office. Theoretically, at least, a guardian agreement provides a solution. As a practical matter, the better solution is to recognize this shortcoming in the practice model and to immediately set out to build a practice or a business with an entity structure and at least one other equity partner (even just a 5 percent owner, for example)—in which case, the role of guardian falls to a partner through the use of a buy-sell or shareholders' agreement as outlined next. Your temporary fill-in is an owner of your business and will have access to the necessary information and authority with the clients and the broker-dealer or custodian, to make good and timely decisions.

In sum, a guardian agreement is best utilized as part of a more comprehensive plan and by partners in a single business. As a financial professional in charge of managing and directing investments to last for at least your clients' lifetimes and usually beyond, you have a duty as an independent owner to build a business to do what you're promising or certainly implying that you'll do. Let's look next at how a professional continuity plan is structured for a financial services or advisory business and how it is integrated into the succession planning process.

Buy-Sell Agreements

For businesses or firms set up as an entity (corporation or limited liability company [LLC]) with two or more owners, the choice of continuity partner is fairly clear—a fellow owner or owners will be the best choice. If a shareholders' agreement or an operating agreement has been entered into, the choice is a matter of contractual obligation. In that a shareholders' agreement refers to a corporation and an operating agreement refers to an LLC, we'll use the more generic term of a *buy-sell agreement* to refer to a continuity planning agreement for multiple owners of a corporation, a partnership, or an LLC.

A buy-sell agreement is a legal document that specifies how a privately held company or its owners will redistribute ownership in the event that one of the owners dies, becomes disabled, retires, or otherwise leaves the business. The agreement is a contractual covenant by each owner (and the company) to redeem or purchase the stake of any owner who departs, with the goal of providing payment of value to that individual or to his or her estate, and to ensure that the business enterprise survives. A buy-sell agreement also helps to reduce the complications of having a surviving spouse (or a son or daughter) or Uncle Charley suddenly appear at the ownership table in the event their loved one dies or becomes disabled.

Note: Before proceeding, it is important to point out that the use of an entity structure does not always create a clear and immediate solution, as many advisors build individual books, using the entity only to share expenses and create some cost savings. The central entity typically has little or no value in this setting and is all but disregarded for continuity and valuation purposes. Partners in these types of arrangements tend to have their own specialties with different revenue models and client demographics than the seller's. Think of a practice model with one partner who is an active portfolio manager, one who is a passive portfolio manager, one who sells insurance products, and one who does hourly or flat fee financial planning work. This dynamic makes it difficult for any of them to buy one of the others' practices or books. Continuity solutions still exist for this model, but are more limited and tend to shift toward the guardian agreement format and/or a fast sale to an experienced local buyer with a very similar revenue model, or even a revenue-sharing arrangement if the book is small enough.

In the case of a privately held, independent financial services business, the primary goal of a buy-sell agreement is to avoid conflict and confusion by keeping ownership and control in the hands of those individuals who will be responsible for managing the operations of the business. In other words, the goal of such an agreement is successful business continuity under less than optimum conditions. As such, the buy-sell agreement is the fallback plan or safety net and is an integral part of a well-designed and longer-range succession plan. While buy-sell agreements are common in most businesses across the spectrum, the continuation of a highly regulated business means this document takes on even greater importance.

A buy-sell agreement also establishes a valuation mechanism and agreed-upon payment terms to facilitate the ownership transfer. This process is actually a "double-edged sword," though, since the valuation approach and payment terms the owners must agree to in advance of the transfer event will determine what any one of the owners or his or her estate might receive upon death or disability; it is also the value that the remaining owner(s) would have to pay for another's shares or ownership interest.

A buy-sell agreement creates a protocol for deciding who will be the buyer of an existing owner's interest. In general, the starting place is stock (or ownership) redemption, followed by the ability to implement a cross-purchase arrangement. If redemption by the company is not the choice by the remaining shareholders upon a triggering event, the second choice is usually the purchase of the exiting owner's interest by all the remaining shareholders on a pro rata basis; this helps to maintain the status quo in a multiple-owner business or firm. If ownership is not redeemed or purchased by the remaining shareholders on a pro rata basis, the next level is usually the purchase by any one of the remaining shareholders. And finally, if none of the previous levels work out, the final level of value realization is to sell the interest to a third party—not practical, but necessary in some instances.

A buy-sell agreement is not a crisis document, or at least it is not intended to be figured out in the midst of a crisis. Rather, it should be a well-
planned agreement, executed in advance, shared with the owners' spouses
and stakeholders (CPA, attorney, etc.), and revisited annually. It is designed
to help shareholders or business partners deal with unpredictable business
situations in the best way possible. At the very least, it provides some
framework for when the parties can't agree on buyout terms.

FUNDING YOUR CONTINUITY PLAN

The default arrangement for a buyout triggered by death or disability is
seller financing over an extended period of time (five to 10 years). In other
words, the buyer, whether it be the company through redemption or one
or more individuals (i.e., the remaining shareholders or partners) through
a cross-purchase arrangement, executes a promissory note and makes payments to the seller or to the estate of the deceased or disabled partner. Do
not use an earn-out arrangement for this type of situation and this length
of financing.

Buy-sell agreements are often triggered on short notice, which practically
results in a very small down payment; frankly, it is hard to maintain a high
level of liquidity in a small business in anticipation of an event you hope
won't ever happen within the context of a pass-through entity structure. The
most common structures just aren't built to save or sit on a lot of extra cash.
A nominal down payment, in turn, will place a heavier load on the cash flow
stream of the business or individual buyer for many years to come, often
on an after-tax basis, and occasionally during the course of a recessionary
event, or upon the loss of one or more large clients (which can, and often
does, follow a triggering event).

For all these reasons, the buyout process can be significantly aided by
proper funding mechanisms such as life insurance or lump-sum disability
insurance. For buyouts triggered by death, a life insurance policy held by
the buyer (many times this is the business itself) on each of the owners
can be an effective option for funding either a down payment or the
entire purchase price. Lump-sum disability insurance is also an option
for buyouts triggered by disability, but the policy is generally aimed at
providing a significant down payment (relying on the acquired cash flow
to pay the balance). Without adequate funding, you may be solving one
serious problem while simultaneously creating a different and equally
serious problem.

Adequately funding a buy-sell agreement requires a high level of
advanced planning and professional guidance. Insurance funding strategies

depend on whether the buyer will be the entity or one or more of the remaining individual shareholders or partners, and what type of entity you have (C corporation, S corporation, or LLC taxed as one of three different models). To obtain the correct answers, you'll need to consider the challenges from legal, tax, regulatory, and cash flow perspectives, and then make decisions based on the talent level left behind to mind the store and handle the obligations. And once you've figured it out, the answers tend to change over time as the business grows and the ownership changes.

Funding also requires an accurate determination of value. Obtain a formal valuation before you set up your continuity plan so that all of the owners can agree on the process and each can live with the results should the agreement be suddenly triggered and under trying circumstances. Do not use a multiple of revenue to accomplish this task; depending on the circumstances of the buyout, as well as the economic climate, you may lock in a payment obligation that is unsustainable and will threaten the business's ability to survive. In this case, simple is not better.

Bank financing is also a solution to consider. It is still difficult and impractical to obtain bank financing from a local institution for the purposes we're talking about here, especially in the context of a highly regulated, intangible, professional services model, but significant progress continues to be made on this front. With proper cash flow modeling, a strong foundational structure, proper valuation techniques, and adequate payment terms, bank financing is a viable solution should your buy-sell agreement be triggered.

CONTINUITY PLAN DOS AND DON'TS

Regardless of the type of continuity agreement you use, here are some pointers that you should consider to ensure that your continuity plan and agreement not only address but also fulfill your intentions and those of your business partners when it is time for a shareholder or member to leave or when disaster strikes.

- DO NOT use a multiple of value or any static formula or a fixed dollar amount (stated value) to determine the value of the business or any owner's share of the business in a continuity plan. When you do this, you are locking in a number that you must pay in the years to come based on the trailing 12 months revenue (or earnings) at the time of the triggering event. For example, what if there was a large one-time annuity sale in the past 12 months that spiked revenue? If you use the trailing 12 months to determine value in the future, then you capture that revenue spike, even though it may not be sustainable moving forward.

Remember what happened in October 2008? Using the trailing 12 months as the determinant of value would have meant that the surviving owners would have had to tackle a number without the revenue streams that supported its calculation. The same thing can happen when a partner who, by way of example, is subject to a regulatory event and causes harm to the company, then suffers a severe heart attack, is disabled, and then has his or her value locked in place just before the revenues take a severe hit. Bad news, but it happens.

- DO NOT guess at the payment terms contracted for in a buy-sell agreement, or simply plug in a number that seems about right. We recommend using a spreadsheet format to calculate the after-tax effects of buying out an exiting partner that also take into account the business's overhead structure, growth rates, cost to replace the lost talent, interest rates, and so on. Remember, one of the goals of a buy-sell agreement is to ensure that the company survives the buyout process. Take the time to do the math.

- DO value your business and review your buy-sell agreement once each year. Log the annual event right now on your Outlook calendar or customer relationship management (CRM) system for the next 10 years. A routine review of the agreement can help business owners ensure that their document takes into account changes in personal circumstances or changes in the business itself, and provides for evolution of the plan and the business valuation mechanism. That way, the agreement will be ready to do the job when you need it most.

- DO focus on and understand the definition of *disability* in your continuity agreement. Many business owners simply trust the standard attorney boilerplate language to define when an owner is disabled and must be bought out or must sell. The reality of most disability cases is not the sudden and completely debilitating, nearly fatal auto accident; instead, it is often something more subtle, some health issue that starts and stops for uneven intervals over many years, or it is the disability or medical condition of an advisor's spouse or child that significantly alters the advisor's involvement and effectiveness on the job. Study the definition in your agreement carefully and make it fit the circumstances of your industry, your business, and your life.

- DO make sure that your agreement addresses what happens in the event of the involuntary departure of one of the partners or shareholders. In instances like these, the treatment of the departing shareholder may depend on the circumstances surrounding the departure. An owner who is asked to leave as a result of a difference in goals and objectives may be viewed very differently than a person who leaves because of performance issues or, even worse, regulatory violations. Draft these considerations as early as possible, while everyone is getting along well and these issues are still merely theoretical.

- DO watch out for the situation where there are two or more senior owners of similar age. An internal buyout arrangement can require as many as seven to 10 years or more to pay off from operational cash flow after taxes and after replacing the exiting advisor owner. This makes the process impractical for a single remaining owner in his or her late 50s or early 60s. One commonly used solution is to set up an internal ownership track that provides an opportunity for the next generation to step in on a continuity basis and purchase the exiting owner's shares or interest, perhaps on a non-pro rata basis.

- DO take the time to learn your options and best strategies, especially if you're a single-owner, one-generational practice model. Signing a revenue-sharing–based continuity agreement might seem easy, but if you end up receiving 30 cents on the dollar, there is very little you can do about it. Consider instead the Practice Emergency Program (PEP), a unique option offered by FP Transitions. Advisors who have not identified a suitable buyer for a continuity agreement or a buy-sell agreement can enroll in PEP and authorize FP Transitions to sell the advisor's business on the open market upon the advisor's death or disability to the best-qualified successor. With a 50:1 buyer-to-seller ratio, it is quite likely that you'll come closer to realizing the value of what you've built than using a revenue-sharing arrangement.

- DO NOT settle for a continuity plan that is only *better than nothing* unless that is how you feel about your clients and what you've spent your career doing. When you get above $200,000 to $250,000 in gross revenue or gross dealer concession (GDC), do the job right. In this day and age, half of a million dollars in value, at long-term capital gains rates, deserves your time and attention.

While none of us wants to believe that our association with our business partners or shareholders may someday come to an end, as it relates to a continuity agreement, it is always good to remember that, one way or another, *you will part ways.* It is important to plan for such events well in advance. On that note, the fact that partnerships end is not a good reason to avoid having a partner; it is a great reason to plan ahead and build something stronger than any one individual.

A POWERFUL ACQUISITION TOOL

When practice owners decide to list and sell their practices on the FP Transitions' listing system, the typical response is about a 50-to-1 buyer-to-seller ratio. From a buyer's perspective, those are long odds indeed. But there is a way to reduce those odds significantly, and literally take the seller off the market years beforehand. Successful and repeat buyers, those who acquire a practice every year, often use an additional approach—they become a continuity partner.

The tools to succeed are simple. Value your business, structure it correctly, and then set up your own continuity plan. Once you've figured out how to do these basic things for yourself, do the same for others who are in your area but smaller than you in terms of value and cash flow. An enduring business model can and should become the continuity partner for five or six other smaller practices in the same geographic area and within the same broker-dealer or custodial network. The arrangement is straightforward. Execute a continuity agreement in which your business agrees to become the continuity partner, and guardian if need be and if possible, for a single-owner practice. And then do it over and over again.

These stand-by arrangements provide the owner of the smaller practice with backup protection, perhaps even a guardian in case of temporary disability, and an obligated buyer to pay fair market value with agreed-upon payment terms at long-term capital gains rates, and even a possible employer for the key staff members. For the prospective seller, this arrangement is far superior to the popular but questionable revenue-sharing approach outlined earlier. Many times, these continuity arrangements lead into more formal succession plans or even mergers with the continuity partner. It's like tying up a couple of life rafts next to your ship.

This solution also provides the single, one-generational practice owner with a great answer to the question clients start asking at some point or another: "What happens to me if something happens to you?"

COMMUNICATING YOUR PLAN

On previous occasions in this book, we've asked you an important question on behalf of your clients: "What happens to me if something happens to you?" Let's answer that question now, and emphatically.

Your answer is (or should be): "I have a plan. I have a long-term plan for this business, which is being built to serve not only you, but your children and grandchildren, and, by the way, I'd like to meet them and help make them a part of your long-term planning process. I also have a short-term plan, just in case I get hit by the proverbial bus. Would you like to know more?"

Once you have the structure in place and you're in the process of building an enduring and strong business, *tell people!* Tell your clients, tell your family, tell your staff, and tell the community! There are too few enduring businesses in this industry—but that is a positive if you're one of the few, one of the shipbuilders. You can offer something to your clients and to future advisor recruits and new hires that a one-owner, one-generational practice can never compete with. You're building something to last and to make a difference.

CHAPTER 6

Charting Your Succession Course

EXIT STRATEGIES VERSUS SUCCESSION PLANS

I fly a lot in my work for FP Transitions—millions of miles, so far. I once asked a pilot, "If the engines of this airliner quit at altitude, say 30,000 feet, how far can we fly before we hit the earth?" The captain said that it would vary depending upon the wind and the load, of course, but around 100 to 110 miles would be a good estimate. This is the same approach that many advisors use toward the end of their careers. Once the engines start to fade, they hold on until the end, keep the ride smooth, and make it last as long as possible. In the absence of all other choices, it's a great plan! It is a tale of survival. In this industry, however, there are usually other and better alternatives than a dead-stick landing.

Every succession plan we design and implement for an independent advisor is unique. No two are exactly alike. While many plans have common assembly components, plans are tailored to every founding or senior advisor's unique goals and needs. Succession plans often center on the founder's need for a lifetime of income and benefits and take into account the founding owner or owners' age(s), health, time frame, business skills, workweek preferences, retirement preferences, and staffing levels and strengths, among other things. There are lots of plans and lots of strategies, but don't confuse a formal plan with an idea, a hope, a prayer, or something that will work itself out later on. This is something that you need to commit to and put in writing, sooner than later.

Succession planning is not about winding down and walking away, or selling what you've built. Selling your practice to the best match for the best price and terms you can get in a seller's market is actually an exit strategy. An exit strategy provides for your clients, helps you monetize your value, but it does bring your practice to a close. The point is, you need to evaluate your current position, the value of what you've built, and decide for yourself what makes the most sense—a succession plan, an exit strategy, or just hanging on as long as you can until it's over. As an independent owner, that decision belongs to you. You've earned that right and we respect that.

Do understand that you don't have to choose one strategy or another; the choices are not mutually exclusive. A comprehensive plan incorporates all possibilities but creates a hierarchy based on goals and resources, and the things you can control, and the things that you can't control. Most of these strategies can and should be linked together to provide flexibility and multiple levels of protection. Most planning exercises begin by valuing the practice or business based on what a third-party buyer would likely pay for it; this not only establishes an equity value number to plan around, but it also makes the fallback plan clearer, at least in terms of a specific number to think about. If selling internally doesn't end up working out, sell the business to the best-qualified third party and work with the new owner for a while until it's time to fully retire. If the math around that prospect still isn't compelling, then glide in from 30,000 feet and call it a day; you'll know full well what the cash flow needs to be to offset the equity number. Along the way, should severe injury or disability be the cause of a sudden change of plans, your continuity plan is designed to step in and address the emergency and provide a clear and alternative path for you and your clients.

More or less, that's how it all works, in a nutshell. So before we consider the best succession planning strategies, let's talk about the best exit strategies, because in this industry, these are often top of mind. There are a number of great options to choose from.

SELLING YOUR PRACTICE

The system for buying and selling practices and transitioning client relationships in this industry is now well established. It is dependable, it is predictable, and it works. If you're looking for the fastest and most efficient exit strategy, look no further.

Selling Externally (to a Third Party)

Transitioning the ownership of a privately and independently owned financial services practice to a third-party buyer or successor has evolved significantly over the past 10 years. Today, independently owned financial services practices have measurable equity, an industry-specific valuation system, and a stream of transaction data on which to base sales and acquisition decisions. Bank financing is also becoming increasingly available from qualified and experienced lenders, though most transactions are still seller financed.

Practice values have been slowly but steadily increasing over the 16 years we've been tracking the data, fueled in part by a strong and stable seller's market. As mentioned, the current buyer-to-seller ratio is about 50 to 1, but we've never seen this result in an auction or a bidding war, at least not on our watch. Instead, advisors go about the process in a very professional manner, one that the client base tends to strongly approve of, at least in hindsight. The first criterion is quality of the match. Sellers prefer to find buyers who are mirror images of themselves, at least in terms of client base, revenue streams, and investment philosophy, but larger in terms of cash flow and value (i.e., businesses tend to buy practices). The second criterion is geography. Sometimes this means a buyer close by, and sometimes it doesn't. A seller who wants to keep his or her office open, the staff employed, and the same brick-and-mortar operation in place will often prefer a buyer who does not have a local presence. A buyer with four months left on the lease and with no intentions of signing another lease will usually prefer a strong local buyer. The last issue is price and terms.

Understanding the dynamics of the deal structuring techniques associated with buying and selling a financial services practice is a prerequisite to understanding equity value. The first mistake that many buyers and sellers make when approaching a transaction is to focus on determining the purchase price without fully considering the underlying deal terms and tax allocations. In the acquisition or sale of a professional services practice, value is inextricably tied to the terms of the deal—the amount of the down payment, the use of contingent financing (such as an earn-out or an adjustable note), the duration of the financing period, the tax allocation strategy, and even the interest rate the seller will charge to finance the transaction.

The most common deal structure is about one-third of the purchase price paid as a nonrefundable down payment, with the balance seller financed over anywhere from three to six years. Typically, the more recurring revenue there is, the larger the down payment and the shorter the financing terms. Seller financing usually contains some type of contingency to make sure that the assets and cash flow actually transfer and can be retained for a period of time. The most commonly used contingent financing method is a performance-based promissory note. Earn-outs are infrequently used these days due to regulatory concerns and licensing issues.

In the marketplace for independent financial services practices selling for less than $10 million, most sales transactions and acquisitions between third parties are structured as asset sales, not stock sales (fee-only practices being the exception to the rule). Conversely, most sales transactions and acquisitions between employers and employees, or between parents and a son or daughter, are stock sales. The differences between these two methods are telling. Asset sales tend to shift control completely, all at once, whereas stock sales can be used to effect a very gradual change of control, sometimes over a period as long as 10 to 20 years. The purchase of assets provides better near-term tax benefits for the buyer. The purchase of stock provides a more gradual transition of ownership and leadership.

The average age of an advisor who sells and walks away (after an appropriate transition period to help the clients get comfortable with the chosen buyer) is about 60. Buyers tend to be in the 45 to 50 years age range. In other words, sellers who choose this strategy are a long way from the attrition model; these are practice owners who aren't just selling what is left, but instead are selling at or close to peak value and are actively participating in choosing their replacement.

From the clients' perspective, the transactions are almost always called mergers regardless of whether that term is legally even in the ballpark. The seller agrees to stay on for up to one year or until the vast majority of the client base is comfortable working with the buyer and his or her staff. Selling to a larger, stronger business also means that most of the seller's key staff members have job opportunities ready and waiting (provided their compensation benchmarks competitively), and it is this overall deal structure that tends to support very high transition and retention rates—when done correctly.

Internal Buyout (Selling Internally to a Partner or Key Employee)

A closely related option is selling the entire practice internally to a son, a daughter, or one or more key employees. To be clear, this option refers to a one-time sale where the ownership of the practice changes hands to a new owner—only the owner was formally part of the same practice. It differs substantially from a succession plan (which we describe at length later) in one important way: The shift in ownership and control takes place all at once and the sale is consummated with a combination of cash and promissory notes. In that regard, its structure is similar to a sale to an outside party. But mechanically it usually doesn't unfold anything like a sale to a third party. Most of the buyers in this category have limited cash reserves and little or no actual experience as owners (don't confuse producers with owners—they are two entirely different things).

Let's reset the table and better understand this unique transition in terms of an exit strategy. Ninety-five percent of today's independent advisors begin the succession planning process as the sole owners of their practice, and somewhere north of that 95 percent number is the percentage of advisor/owners who haven't been anyone's employee in the past 20 years. That's to say, this probably isn't a good time to start learning how to work for someone else. That's okay, because a similar percentage of next-generation advisors who are currently employees have never been owners of a small business before, so in some sense, this is a match made in heaven; both sides need each other to succeed in reaching their goals. But if that is the case, and if time is not an immediate issue, it is probably better to use a succession structure, as we will describe later.

Most sales of this type that we see are as a result of an event: the death or disability of the owner of the practice. Less frequently, a life change, the illness of a spouse, or an employment or business opportunity that requires an immediate sale, and the first buyers to come forward happen to be part of the practice. This is not always the best solution, and often is the worst solution financially, but it may seem the most expedient at the time.

The range of structuring options is usually rather narrow for these kinds of internal sales. Internal sales tend to take either of two forms: (1) the sale of assets or (2) the sale of stock (or ownership interests in an LLC). If the practice is structured as a sole proprietorship (about 20 percent of the practices and businesses we value in this industry are set up this way), the options narrow even more. A sole proprietorship can only sell assets, whereas the corporation or LLC can generally choose to sell assets or stock.

In an asset sale, there are two more variations. One is the sell and walk away or fade away form, which is self-evident, and the second is a partial book sale. The problem, to be blunt, is that the internal buyer usually doesn't have the money or the experience to step in and take over an established practice or business that quickly. So let's focus on the more common approach—a partial book sale. The owner literally divides his or her client list into halves or thirds and then sells a partial list to the younger internal advisor. The purchase is financed on a promissory note with one adjustment period (just in case) for about three years and, if all goes well, the next batch of clients, or the other half, is sold on similar terms.

The partial book approach allows the two advisors to work side by side, but as two separate businesses. The name of the owner's business can be shared as a "dba" or trade name by the two sole proprietors who each run their books as they please, work the hours they choose, and earn the pay they earn. From the clients' perspective, outside looking in, it's the same practice it has always been. The seller helps the buyer and the clients gradually adjust to the changes over time, and transition risk is minimal. The transaction is never positioned as a sale but rather as a merger or, better yet, "the early stages of a well-designed and thoughtful succession plan designed to provide the clients' and their children and grandchildren with continuing services for generations to come." Maybe it is, and maybe it isn't.

As these two practices are run side by side, but separately, they are contractually linked with a continuity agreement. The formal continuity agreement says that the junior advisor will step in and be obligated to purchase the rest of the founder's practice in the event of the founder's death or disability. The junior advisor would also have first dibs on the remaining clients and assets in the founder's practice in the event of early retirement.

More often than not, however, our one-owner practice scenario has a wrinkle in it: The junior advisor has been compensated with a revenue-sharing arrangement and has built his or her own small book under the owner's roof. This isn't bad or good for internal selling purposes, but it is something most independent advisors have to deal with. In some cases, we end up performing two separate valuations and literally treat the two books as two separate practices, even though the clients see it as just one business. In this case, what is being sold is the value of the founder's book unless the junior advisor feels otherwise.

An asset sale is one way to get the job done, and that is the common pattern in a sale to a third party. But as you've learned, most third-party buyers are larger and stronger than the sellers they acquire, so paying 30 percent to 40 percent cash down and financing the balance over three or four years is easy. Internal buyers rarely have the means to compete with better-capitalized outside buyers, and that limits the practicality of this approach as an exit strategy. That said, internal buyers have a different edge: familiarity with the clients and the owner. They don't have to compete, but they do need some special financing to get the deal done, and that is where succession planning often reenters the picture in the form of an incremental sale over time.

Internal ownership plans that utilize a stock sale approach do so for a different reason: The participating advisors prefer to be co-owners of the same business, usually for an extended period of time. Internal transitions using a stock sale (or ownership interests in an LLC) as part of a succession plan are designed around a very gradual sale of ownership and transfer of responsibilities (10 to 20 years is the norm). This is a great way to take the step up from a practice to a multigenerational, enduring business, but this step requires more planning, time, effort, and sophistication than the straight internal buyout we have just described.

For clarity, let's keep these options simple and separate. If you are looking to sell and walk away and your first choice for a buyer is a trusted employee or son or daughter, then the internal buyout plan works. If instead the transaction needs time to develop and for them to grow into the role of an owner, to gather the funds, and to assure you of their ability to run the business in the long run and generate the money needed to pay off the debts that a buyout would incur, then we are speaking about a succession plan and *not* an internal buyout.

The benefits of an internal succession plan versus an internal buyout are these: (1) As a founder, you have the opportunity to hire, train, and work with your chosen successor for many years before retirement; (2) the junior partner is well known to the client base and the practice's referral sources; and (3) the retiring owner can retire on the job, remain in control of his or her own practice, and ensure that the client base is well taken care of for the duration. The internal successor's lack of money can actually become a positive in this plan. The well-financed external buyer expects immediate control of the operations; the junior advisor is often glad to have a built-in, part-time mentor for many years who relinquishes control as the successor is ready to take over the reins, and that this comes with long-term, low-interest, friendly financing (i.e., the seller!) is even better.

Something Different: The GlidePath Strategy

We opened this chapter by distinguishing between an exit strategy and a succession plan. The GlidePath strategy falls somewhere in between. The GlidePath strategy, pioneered by FP Transitions, is unique and serves to accomplish several goals by combining a liquidity event with allowing the advisor to stay on and continue to work as long as he or she wants to or can. The plan blends or merges a smaller practice into a larger and similar business model in order to create an equity realization event, a continuity plan, and an ongoing employment opportunity with appropriate compensation. Here is how it works.

Let's call our seller "Becky." Becky is 68 years old. Becky's practice is structured as an LLC and is taxed as a disregarded entity; she is the sole owner and has been for the past 34 years. Becky has her practice valued in order to start thinking about what she wants to do in the next couple of years, and the valuation results come in at $1,140,000.

Selling and walking away is not an option because Becky isn't ready to stop working, and even so, she would like at least a couple of more years of income before she does so. But Becky also is worried about some personal health issues that might necessitate an earlier and more rapid exit. Some days this seems like an issue out on the horizon, but other days it feels more like the sword of Damocles. Enter the GlidePath strategy.

The GlidePath strategy starts with a valuation of the subject practice. Once the value is determined, a search for a merger partner is undertaken. In most cases, applicants are numerous and of high quality, at least in a competitive open marketplace. Becky chooses a local firm about three times her size in terms of cash flow and value and sells her practice to this firm under a special GlidePath arrangement and documentation package. As a part of this process, a complete list of Becky's clients and prospects and referral sources is attached to the list of assets she is transitioning. The buyer agrees to pay a nonrefundable down payment to Becky of $300,000, and executes a promissory note for the balance. Most of these monies are taxed at long-term capital gains rates to Becky. The merger partner then enters into an employment agreement with Becky.

During the term of the employment agreement, Becky will receive a base salary and incentive payments for new client referrals, but interest-only payments on the balance owed. At the conclusion of year 3, it becomes obvious that Becky's health condition is growing more serious and she needs to stop working and focus more attention on her own issues, so Becky provides a six-month notice that she is going to fully retire. On the eve of retirement, the revenue of Becky's practice is reviewed once more and it is determined that it has been sustained. Only seven clients were lost during the transition period, but the loss of these clients and assets was more than offset by increased investments of the remaining client base under the combined care of the merged businesses and the addition of several new and larger clients.

The sustained value is reflected on an adjustable promissory note divided into 60 equal monthly payments, and six months later, the payments begin as Becky settles into retirement. Becky's former clients have had more than enough time to get used to the new firm during the past three and a half years (with Becky always in the background to ease the transition process). And for the duration, Becky had an emergency continuity plan ready, just in case, built into the structure of the deal—one that would help her realize almost 100 percent of the value she had built.

The GlidePath strategy is an excellent illustration of how the various elements and benefits of a succession plan, an exit strategy, a continuity plan, and even the tactical advantages of a competitive seller's market can, and often are, blended together to fashion a great solution for founder, acquirer/successor, staff, clients, and the families of all the aforementioned parties. It is important that you not think one-dimensionally when considering your options. The operative term in the title of this book is *Planning*, and, as you tell your clients, with a good plan, good information, and enough time, almost anything is possible.

MERGERS

Merger is a great word in the field of the succession planning professional! It is used often and for good reason. This term is applied to everything from a sale to an acquisition, or to the GlidePath strategy in the preceding section, or to an actual, legal, tax-free reorganization under Section 368 of the Internal Revenue Code. *Merger* is a term that implies growth, success, forward progress, strength, and endurance—things every business owner loves to hear or think about and wants to tell others about. And that's why everybody uses the *merger* term, regardless of what actually transpired.

But let's not ignore the formal approach and what this term and related terms actually mean to those with a professional, legal, or tax background. By the book, a merger is the joining together of two previously separate companies into a single economic entity. A merger is formally defined as the statutory combination of two or more corporations, in which one of the corporations survives and the other corporation ceases to exist. In a true merger, the owners or leaders of the merged businesses are typically retained for at least several years.

An acquisition, in contrast, is taking possession of another business through the purchase of its stock or assets. Acquisitions are also called takeovers or buyouts. All acquisitions involve one firm purchasing another. In the financial services industry, at least at the small market capitalization level, the owner(s) of the acquired practice is/are commonly removed from the equation following a brief postclosing transition period. In most cases, they're too expensive to keep on board, and two entrepreneurs who are accustomed to calling the shots is a difficult marriage to sustain.

An acquisition is a taxable transaction. Following the acquisition of another company's assets, the buyer can record the acquired assets at their fair market value (usually much greater than the seller's tax basis), thereby yielding more depreciation to the buyer. The seller, in turn, must pay taxes on the difference between the consideration received and the seller's basis in the business (which is usually nominal). Following the acquisition of another company's stock, the buyer has basis in the investment while the seller typically receives long-term capital gains tax treatment.

In a merger, certain exchanges of stock are considered tax-free reorganizations, which permit the owners of one company to exchange their shares for the stock of the acquirer without paying taxes. In order to qualify as a nontaxable event, the Internal Revenue Code (IRC) stipulates that the following four requirements (among others) be met:

1. The transaction must have a bona fide "business purpose" other than tax avoidance.
2. There must be a continuity of ownership interest, where at least 50 percent of the consideration is paid through the acquirer's stock.
3. There must be continuity of the business enterprise, where the buyer must either continue the seller's historic business or use a significant proportion of the acquired assets in the business.
4. The transaction cannot be part of a larger plan that, in its entirety, constitutes a taxable acquisition.

The Internal Revenue Service (IRS) has included these basic requirements into four types of legal reorganizations, commonly described as type

A, B, C, or D reorganizations. The letter designations come from the paragraph letters in the IRC (Section 368) under which they are described.

These mergers require a legal professional with a strong tax background, and can be complicated from the layman's perspective, which of course means they are fairly expensive as well. It isn't the cost factor that makes actual, honest-to-goodness mergers rare, though; it is more about the challenges of integrating two cultures, two leadership styles, and two workforces. We work with several thousand independent financial services and advisory firms every year ranging in value from $150,000 to over $25 million, and it is rare that we observe a formal IRC merger process at this level.

WHAT DOESN'T WORK IN THIS INDUSTRY

Maybe just as important as exploring your options is offering a few cautionary words from our experience on what does *not* work. Most of these lessons were learned by watching our clients do it the wrong way and listening to their stories about the consequences. There are no monopolies on good ideas, and new strategies in succession will always be evolving—and we hope to be leading the charge—but some old methods definitely need to be discarded. Here is what doesn't work (which tends to focus on compensation-based strategies as opposed to equity-based strategies), a list that, by virtue of previous discussion, must include the use of revenue-sharing arrangements.

Granting of Ownership

Rule No. 1: Do not give away your business. Don't create a new owner in your business by presenting someone a gift of stock; it isn't a birthday present, and the IRS stands in the background nodding its head in agreement.

Rule No. 2: If you're going to ignore Rule No. 1, then sell stock first and most, and grant stock second and least. As you read on and learn more about stock grants in the following chapter under "The Nuts and Bolts of a Plan," you'll come to appreciate those terms of art and understand how they will help you and your succession team assemble a state-of-the-art succession plan.

That said, it is not unusual for owners of independent financial services businesses to seek to reward key staff members with a grant of stock or ownership interests. Granting seems so simple, quick, and paperless. How hard can it be to give some shares of stock in an intangible, professional services business to a deserving employee, son, or daughter? It often creates (or cements) a special bond between owner and employee, soon to be partner; obviously that holds true between parent and son or daughter. What's the big deal?

In short, the answer is "taxes." This part of the game is rigged against you and you can learn more as you keep reading, but there is a possible way through this minefield, a way to strategically employ stock grants in a tax-efficient and business-strengthening manner.

To that end, most stock grants involve gradually or incrementally issuing the shares (or units in an LLC) over time, based on a promise that ties the reward to tenure or some other measurable achievement. Instead of or in addition to a cash bonus, consider a stock bonus. This approach has the benefit of the recipient being able to rely on the growing profit distributions from previously purchased shares to help the minority owner address the tax costs associated with the grant (otherwise, a cash bonus will be needed). Finally, discounts for lack of control (for minority ownership interests) and lack of marketability (for ownership interests in privately held companies) applied to the cash value of the shares can also be used to minimize the tax burden.

In sum, the granting or awarding of stock to one or more key employees can be an important part of a comprehensive succession plan and an owner's level compensation strategy when used properly. But it needs to be part of a plan, and not the plan itself.

Phantom Stock Plans

A phantom stock plan (PSP) is not a succession strategy. It is not even an exit strategy. It is a compensation tool.

Phantom stock plans are a useful and valuable planning tool in the right context. A PSP is actually a compensation strategy in which a business promises to pay cash at some future date in an amount equal to the market value of a number of shares of its stock. Thus, the payout will increase if the stock price (based on the value of the independent financial services or advisory business) rises, and will decrease if the value of the stock falls, but without the PSP participant actually receiving any real stock. Conversely, the PSP participant has no indebtedness or similar obligation as is the case with an advisor who actually invests money into an ownership position or who signs a promissory note.

Just to be clear, rather than getting physical stock, the employee or PSP participant receives pretend stock. Even though it's not real, the phantom stock follows the price movement of the business's actual stock, which can be determined through an annual valuation of the business, for example. The valuation results are shared with all PSP participants.

Like other forms of stock-based compensation plans (see Figure 6.1), phantom stock broadly serves to encourage employee retention, and to

COMPENSATION-BASED STRATEGIES
- STOCK APPRECIATION RIGHTS
- PHANTOM STOCK
- STOCK OPTION PLANS
- PROFIT-SHARING PLAN
- PROFITS INTEREST (LLCs)
- DEFERRED COMPENSATION PLAN
- DEFINED BENEFITS PLAN

FIGURE 6.1 Compensation-Based Strategies

align the interests of participants and actual shareholders or owners. PSP participants are typically employees, but may also be directors, third-party vendors, or others. Phantom stock is essentially a cash bonus plan, although some plans pay out the benefits in the form of actual shares. Every PSP is unique and can be custom drafted to fit the circumstances and goals of the business owners and PSP participants. If you are Financial Industry Regulatory Authority (FINRA) regulated and you want to have a nonlicensed, nonproducing key employee participate in the benefits of ownership, PSPs are often a great solution.

For accounting purposes, phantom stock is treated in the same way as deferred cash compensation. As the amount of the liability changes each year, an entry is made for the amount accrued. A decline in value would reduce the liability. (This is yet another reason why our more sophisticated clients, those building enduring and transferable businesses, have annual valuations performed.) These entries are not contingent on vesting. Phantom stock payouts are taxable to the employee as ordinary income and deductible to the company. However, they are also subject to complex rules governing deferred compensation that, if not properly followed, can lead to tax penalties.

Many of our clients' attorneys recommend PSPs as a way to retain next-generation talent, to pay above-average compensation for above-average performance, and to help everyone think like an owner without actually having any real partners. If you've ever had a bad partner, you have to appreciate this advice. But let's circle back to the goal of a succession plan: It is to build an enduring business, one capable of outliving you and prospering even as you retire on the job, and to do that, you need real partners, not pretend partners. PSPs have their place, but if you want to end your career as a single owner, then your practice will end with you; pretend ownership makes for a pretend succession plan.

EMPLOYEE STOCK OWNERSHIP PLANS

There is a reason that employee stock ownership plans (ESOPs) occupy this particular place in this book, somewhere between "what doesn't work" and "what does work." ESOPs offer a unique opportunity, to be sure, but it is an approach that doesn't work well for a lot of advisors and for various reasons. After you learn more about this avenue, we'll share our conclusion and observations at the end.

The term *employee stock ownership plan* was first defined by federal legislation in the Employee Retirement Income Security Act (ERISA) of 1974. That makes an ESOP a relatively new form of plan that has been in existence only since September 2, 1974, when ERISA was enacted into law. Yes, when you enact an ESOP, you add one more federal regulator to your list (the U.S. Department of Labor)—not a reason to dismiss this planning strategy, but something many of our clients think about in an already highly regulated industry.

Many ESOPs existed prior to 1974, even though such plans were not defined by federal statute. Employee stock ownership plans were first recognized by the Internal Revenue Service in 1952, but the concept of employee stock ownership plans has been a part of our law since 1921 in the form of stock bonus plans. Stock bonus plans, like ESOPs, are tax-exempt trusts that are designed to enable employees to own part or all of the company they work for without investing their own funds. The distinguishing feature of an ESOP is that an ESOP, unlike a stock bonus plan, may engage in leveraged purchases of company stock. That is, an ESOP not only may acquire stock on a year-by-year basis, but also may borrow funds (usually personally guaranteed by the owner) in order to purchase a block of stock. Historically, ESOPs have tended to be used by C corporations, though S corporations also qualify and now use them frequently as well. ESOPs cannot be used by limited liability companies.

An ESOP is a kind of employee benefit plan, similar in some ways to a profit-sharing plan. In an ESOP, a company sets up a trust fund, into which it contributes new shares of its own stock or cash to buy existing shares. Alternatively, the ESOP can borrow money to buy new or existing shares of its stock, with the company making cash contributions to the plan to enable it to repay the loan. Regardless of how the plan acquires stock, company contributions to the trust are tax deductible, within certain limits, a major plus for this strategy.

According to the National Center for Employee Ownership (NCEO), there are approximately 11,000 employee stock ownership plans (ESOPs) and stock bonus plans covering more than 10 million employees in the United States. The NCEO estimates that an additional 10 million employees participate in plans that provide stock options or other forms of individual equity to most or all employees. Up to five million employees participate in 401(k) plans that are primarily invested in employer stock. As many as 11 million employees buy shares in their employer through employee stock purchase plans. Eliminating overlap, the NCEO estimates that approximately 28 million employees participate in a formal employee ownership plan in one form or another.

Those are impressive numbers, but how do they apply to independent financial services professionals and advisors? For practical purposes, it depends on the size of the business or firm. Here are some general guidelines to consider before an ESOP even starts to enter into the picture:

- Employee payroll is $1 million per year or more.
- Succession management is in place and strong (an ESOP does not create a succession plan).
- Business value is $5 million or more.
- Staffing consists of at least 15 employees.
- Must be a C corporation, S corporation, or willing to switch to one of these two entity structures.

Accepting these general guidelines means that ESOPs are probably a consideration for less than 1 percent of today's independent financial services and advisory practices; adding another federal regulator to your oversight list and being willing to pay the cost of setting up and maintaining an ESOP cuts that number by more than half. In sum, we don't see many ESOPs in the practices, businesses, and firms we work with. But we have many clients who do surpass the levels just listed, so this strategy bears further exploration and explanation.

Why would an independent advisor or financial services professional take the ESOP route? Look at some of the major research on ESOPs for a quick answer. Various studies by the NCEO, the U.S. General Accountability Office, Rutgers University, the University of Washington, and many others come to a consistent conclusion: Companies with an ESOP grow faster and more sustainably than businesses without a formal employee ownership plan. The culture of ownership is a key to increased productivity in an ESOP company. One specific example found that what would have been a 10 percent annual growth rate became a 15 percent growth rate in an ESOP company in which there existed a strong ownership culture (i.e., one in which a broad base of employees felt empowered as co-owners).

ESOPs also enjoy a number of tax and financial advantages not available through other types of plans or strategies:

- If the ESOP acquires 30 percent or more of the outstanding stock of a privately held company, any capital gains tax on the transaction is deferred indefinitely, provided that the seller reinvests the proceeds in "qualified replacement property" within 12 months of the date of sale.

- Unlike a sale or merger, the ESOP enables the seller to sell any portion of his or her stock. A sale or merger usually requires the seller to transfer 100 percent of the control.
- The ESOP enables the company to repay principal with tax-deductible dollars.
- Dividends paid on stock held by an ESOP are fully tax deductible, provided that such dividends either are passed through to ESOP participants or are used to make principal or interest payments on an ESOP loan.
- An ESOP enables an owner to keep control until he or she is ready to fully retire. When the owner does retire, the ESOP enables the owner to pass control to his or her key employees.
- An ESOP can be used to enable a company to make acquisitions of other companies with tax-deductible dollars. In addition, by using an ESOP, the sellers can receive their proceeds tax-free under IRC Section 1042.

ESOPs are most commonly used to provide a market for the shares of a departing owner of a successful, privately held business and, in the process, to motivate and reward employees and to take advantage of incentives to borrow money for acquiring new assets with pretax dollars. In almost every case, ESOPs constitute a contribution to the employees, not an employee purchase, and therein lies the issue with using an ESOP to create a succession plan. Employees become the "beneficial owners" of the stock, but not the legal owners.

Most first-generation, independently owned financial services or advisory practices survive using the "strong man" or, more politically correct, the "strong person" approach. One owner, the founder, typically makes everything happen from production to marketing to sales to servicing, at least for much of the first generation of ownership. As the staff grows and takes on some of those key roles, one thing never changes in most practice models: The founder continues to power the engine of revenue production. Shifting that responsibility and power to the next generation is not something that can be accomplished by an ESOP. Production, the ability to make money for your business, is a skill, and it has to be learned and earned. In this industry, in our experience, ownership follows this process; it does not lead it.

And one more important consideration: According to the NCEO, an ESOP often costs $50,000 or more to set up and run in the first year, and, for most companies "with under a few hundred people, $15,000 to $30,000 annually" to support. Annual valuations are required and the typical cost is around $7,500; sometimes more than one valuation is needed per year, depending on when the actual stock transactions occur. The ESOP plan itself bears a separate cost (usually starting at around $25,000, with five-year updates required), and the transaction documents add yet another layer of cost. Plans may also incur costs for administrators, trustees, and liability insurance, among other things. By comparison, the cost of setting up and maintaining a Lifestyle Succession Plan (explained in the next section) is about one-tenth of these costs, with similar (perhaps superior) benefits.

For all these reasons, we don't see many ESOPs in use by independent financial services professionals, at least at valuation levels of $25 million or less. The sustainable growth benefits enabled by an ESOP are real, but can be accomplished with other strategies that encourage and reward internal, next-generation ownership through direct investment in the business where the next generation of advisors work and produce—perhaps not on as great a tax-advantaged basis, but with other financing and growth advantages. ESOPs support the building of enduring and stable businesses, but they do not directly address or resolve the issue of succession planning.

WHAT DOES WORK? A LIFESTYLE SUCCESSION PLAN

One of the most efficient and potentially lucrative methods of building an enduring business model and accomplishing a succession of leadership is to help the next generation build on the success and value created by the preceding generation—to turn producers or advisors into investors in a founding owner's legacy. A "Lifestyle Succession Plan" refers to a specific type of internal ownership planning process that reflects the way most advisors work, live, and eventually retire as independent financial services practice owners (see Figure 6.2 for an example). It is a sophisticated planning process in that it is set up to run continually for a decade or more in most cases, but not complicated in that it typically involves just a handful of owners and just one class of voting stock.

A Lifestyle Succession Plan sets up a gradual transition from one generation to the next, designed to support and reward the evolution of business skill sets at the founder level from entrepreneur, to shareholder, to CEO, to mentor. Rest assured that the title refers to a common process and set of assembly tools that can create hundreds of different plans; this is not a "succession plan in a box," nor is there any such thing. A Lifestyle Succession Plan is designed around the founder's goals and needs. (The reference to "EMS" in Figure 6.2 is to the Equity Management System, part of an ongoing maintenance and support program for the founder and his or her succession team that provides annual valuations and benchmarking data, among other things.)

A minority stock or ownership interest is preferably sold to one or more next-generation advisors in the first part of the plan, designated as Tranche 1. The purchase is usually at a small discount, paid for on a long-term note, and can be supplemented with a small, staged grant of stock to reward and encourage longevity of employment. Most Lifestyle Succession Plans are built around this tranche strategy, with each tranche taking about five to seven years to complete, and most plans employ more than one tranche

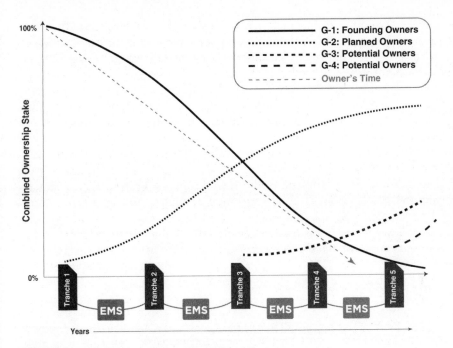

FIGURE 6.2 Lifestyle Succession Plan Schematic

(the nature of an enduring business). This step-by-step approach allows the founder to move gradually but definitively and to alter course if need be.

Retirement for an entrepreneur is rarely a hard stop; usually, most advisors prefer a gradual, on-the-job retirement from five days a week down to four days, down to three days per week, and so on as they get older. This retirement preference serves as the foundation for the Lifestyle Succession Plan strategy. This unique and popular plan, first offered by FP Transitions about six years ago, is designed to reflect the values and needs of the founders—control, flexibility, a return on investment, a client-centered approach, and the ability to build an enduring and transferable business. It also reflects the abilities and resources of next-generation advisors who have the energy, ambition, and skills to form a succession team and have a career to invest in the opportunity. Each party brings strengths to the ownership table.

The Lifestyle Succession Planning process purposefully unfolds slowly and gradually, at least at first, and includes a stage we call the incubator to test the merits of the plan and the next generation of talent that chooses to invest in your business with their money and their careers. Do they want this opportunity as badly as you did? Do they have what it takes to be an owner? Are they willing to invest their careers in the process and put that in writing? This plan is designed to help find out the answers to those questions.

The typical goals in Tranche 1 are to shift from a 100 percent/0 percent ownership ratio (G-1/G-2) to somewhere in the range of 80 percent/20 percent, with the 20 percent owned cumulatively by the G-2 team. Tranche 2 tends to be more in the 70 percent/30 percent or 60 percent/40 percent range, but it depends on the number of tranches, the time frame for the plan, the amount and level of talent available, and many other things. A controlling interest by G-1 should be maintained until he or she spends more time out of the office than in.

The primary thrust behind the Lifestyle Succession Plan is the utilization of all of the compensation elements of a business: wages or paychecks for work performed, profit distributions as a return on investment, and the simultaneous gradual realization of equity value as it grows. Adding an ongoing equity component to a firm's existing compensation structure allows the business to create a shared-risk/shared-reward relationship between employers and employees—a connection between the generations, providing both the means and the rewards of ownership literally, for generations of advisors and their clients to come.

GOALS OF A LIFESTYLE SUCCESSION PLAN

The general goals of a Lifestyle Succession Plan are to help the founder or senior owners realize the value of what they've spent a lifetime building, while simultaneously creating an enduring source of advice and service to the client base. The planning process creates and champions a pathway to ownership, which makes this vehicle a powerful recruiting tool for advisors who want to invest their careers into a business that will be there for the long run.

The more specific goals of this planning process depend on the founder and his or her circumstances and needs, but tend to support a very practical approach to building an independent and enduring financial services business:

- Build strong, sustainable growth.
- Create a focus on the bottom line.
- Implement a practical and reliable continuity plan.
- Design an income-perpetuation strategy for the founding owner.

The process of transforming a one-generational practice into an enduring business isn't normally the purview of the succession planning process, but if these tasks aren't attended to earlier in your career, you may consider it an added bonus of the succession planning process. The attainment of these goals is a joint venture in that success depends on both current and future generations working together, but that also means there is something in this for both sides. It is a shared-risk, shared-reward strategy.

In a large, publicly traded company, the primary objective of management is to build shareholder value. Over the course of the past 10 years, as the equity in a privately held financial services business has steadily grown into the largest, most valuable asset most advisors own, the role of strategically building shareholder value has emerged as the key to this succession planning strategy. Generating strong, sustainable growth is necessary because one of the goals is to attract and retain next-generation advisors—generally, people don't invest in a business that is in decline. In addition, the cash flow generated by sustained future growth is a big part of the answer to the question: "Where does the money come from to buy out the founder?"

This planning process includes gradually shifting everyone at the ownership level from a revenue-sharing and singular-production mentality to a profit-driven business with a new generation of owners who think about production and profitability in the same breath—in other words, next-generation advisors who learn to think like owners because the business profits are tied directly to their investment and their take-home pay. The goal isn't to change the way successful advisors do their business, but rather to add another dimension to the cash flow model—profit distribution checks. This isn't smoke and mirrors, or just another line on your tax return. Owners of businesses should get paid for two things: (1) the work they perform and (2) the investment they've made. Those are separate functions. Businesses need to provide a return on that investment, and that is not what a paycheck is for.

One of the biggest threats to a small business with one owner is not the lack of a succession or retirement plan for the founding owner, but the lack of a plan to protect the clients and the owner's value in the event of the owner's sudden death or disability (temporary or permanent). As noted in the previous chapter, creating a practical and reliable continuity plan for a one-owner, highly regulated professional practice is very challenging. The Lifestyle Succession Plan process makes this process much easier by creating a small but invested ownership team. An internal ownership plan, once implemented, is the best continuity plan available as clients' needs are addressed by other principals of the same business.

Many Lifestyle Succession Plans center on an income-perpetuation strategy, but every plan is unique and custom tailored to the founding owner's age, goals, health, time frame, workweek trajectory, and profitability, and the level of next-generation talent available. For most investment professionals, the reward to be earned from a lifetime of work does not focus on a lump-sum payment derived from selling the business and walking away. Instead, the reward often results from the benefits of perpetuating their business while creating an ongoing stream of income for 10 to 20 years past the typical retirement age. The income-perpetuation strategy is also the result of the very gradual buy-in process by G-2 and G-3 advisors; in a way, the benefit of this process extends to all owners, past, present, and future.

But to be sure, this process takes time, so plan ahead and start early (about age 50 for most advisors is perfect). The reward for doing so is two-fold: (1) You'll remain at the helm of your business longer while working less, and (2) the effective value received can be upwards of five to seven times the trailing 12 months gross revenue based on the starting point for the plan (including equity and profit distributions)—a fair return on your investment of time and leadership. The final, effective value derived by selling equity incrementally, internally, in a growing business is significantly higher than a single open market transaction to an outside party.

What if it doesn't work? First, it is important to acknowledge that failure is indeed a possibility. Internal ownership plans are not without risk and the possibility of unanticipated results. The best approach is to plan well in advance, and leave yourself with options.

If the plan fails, or, said more correctly, if the founder(s) and next-generation advisors do not succeed in transitioning the entire business internally over time from one generation to the next, an external sale or merger remains a distinct possibility. That said, if the plan succeeds only in growing or stabilizing the business and providing continuity protection for temporary disabilities or interruptions in the founder's ability to run the business day in and day out, some very important tasks will have been accomplished.

A Lifestyle Succession Plan is about much more than just succession planning. Integrating multiple generations of talent, and focusing that talent around one business and one shared vision, has the ability not only to perpetuate a business, but to lift that enterprise to an entirely new and higher level of service, achievement, and value. That is good for all the stakeholders.

THE FAMILY BUSINESS—A SPECIAL CASE

In most of this book, I share the collective wisdom of a group of really smart people that I have the pleasure of working alongside every day. This section is a bit different, and more personal, and that's kind of how it is with a multigenerational family business. I have personal experience with this category and, honestly, it has not always gone well. Some days I think I'm the luckiest guy in the world to be able to work with family members, and then other days, well, I swear I'd never do it again. As I write this, I'm leaning toward a family-like business as the best solution.

Businesses aren't perfect, and neither are families, so both have something in common to build around. I've learned that the best approach is to temper expectations, learn from good information and other experienced family business owners, and wade on in with a plan that you adjust frequently. If everyone works at it (parents, children, nieces, nephews, and the other staff members), it can be magical, but that's a big "if."

Family business succession is the process of transitioning management and ownership to the next generation of family members. It is possible that a transition will be triggered by the sudden death, disability, or retirement of the founder (which is the purpose of a continuity plan and agreement), but most formal plans are process driven rather than event driven. Implementation of a successful plan, to family members or others, is often first centered on a gradual transition of key management duties, and later includes a gradual transition of ownership to a team of successors over a five- to 20-year time frame. All of these contributing factors lead to one conclusion: These are almost always incremental sales of stock in a corporation or ownership interests in an LLC or partnership.

It is important to understand that the succession planning process is about far more than just whom to leave the business to and when. At the family business level, most founders or senior owners have equity value that is close to or well in excess of the million-dollar mark (perhaps several million dollars is more appropriate); as a result, most owners/parents can't afford to give the business away, and wouldn't want to if they could. But more important, family businesses of any size almost always depend on nonfamily talent to keep things running smoothly, and nonfamily talent is usually part of the succession planning process. A financial advisory business has serious obligations to fulfill and a demanding client base, many of whom are much older than the next-generation advisors and family members who form the succession team.

So how do you successfully build a multigenerational family business and create a legacy in this industry? Here are some of the most important lessons we've learned from firsthand experience:

- It's about talent first and foremost. Building an enduring and valuable family business in a highly regulated industry may take more talent than the founder has sons, daughters, or relatives to call upon. As such, an important part of building a family business may include the consideration of nonfamily talent as ownership prospects. This doesn't have to terminate the "family" element of the business; adding the necessary skill sets around the namesake family member(s) often makes for a stronger, more competitive business. In fact, at some point, it is often inevitable. Consider reframing the goal as we did at FP Transitions, to building a "family-like business," rewarding the skills of both related and unrelated professionals over the course of a formal plan.

- Make sure everyone understands the distinction between opportunity and entitlement. Successful family businesses must ensure that future generations clearly understand what the family business can do for them, and what the obligations and risks of ownership are in return.

- Create an ownership track early in the business's life cycle and make the ability to become an owner a part of the business culture. Make sure that compensation to family members and nonfamily members is paid at competitive levels, a function best accomplished by annually benchmarking the business against peers, and sharing these benchmarks with managers and key staff members.

- Don't make the common mistake of concluding that a given family member isn't an entrepreneur like the founder of the business. Building on top of a seven-figure business value requires a very different skill set than starting a business from scratch. Building a business, certainly a multigenerational family business, usually benefits from a team of owners who each bring a unique skill set and cumulatively guide the business to a higher level of production and expertise in a collaborative fashion.

- The business has to grow. Without top-line revenue growth and competitive profit margins, the business will die on its own, or be overtaken eventually by better-prepared and better-equipped competitors. Sustained and steady growth in revenue, clients, assets, and even skills from one generation to the next must be part of the ongoing process. In the financial services industry, this is more than just common sense. Since most internal successors and family members don't have sufficient cash reserves to buy into the ownership level on a cash basis, it will be your succession plan that is tasked with answering the key question: "Where does the money come from?" In short, the best answer is future business growth over many years, preferably from two or more next-generation advisors/owners—widen the base of ownership and make time work for you.

- If your goal as a parent (or other relative) is to give stock or ownership to a son, daughter, or relative as part of an estate-planning or a tax-planning strategy, do so through a comprehensive, long-term succession plan. It is a common practice in most family business succession plans to include strategies that involve a sale of stock augmented by a granting strategy over time as the advisor/owner proves his or her commitment to the process. Remember that this is a business with demanding clients, and regardless of how easy it may be to acquire or receive the reins of control and ownership as a family member, management and leadership have to be able to compete for those same clients every day with owners of other financial services businesses that have had to pay for and earn every last client and nickel of revenue the hard way.

- Address value and valuation issues early in the process. For most founders, their financial services business is their largest, most valuable asset, and it represents a lifetime of work. The starting point for a family business succession plan is a formal third-party valuation. This is a critical step—and learning tool—for both sides of the transaction, and even for nonowner siblings. Do not make the mistake of performing the first and only valuation on the eve of retirement or guessing at the value; instead, create a library of annual valuation results to monitor the business's growth over time. Put history and evidence on your side by starting this process early and sharing these results with managers, key staff, and family members, and make equity value part of your business culture.

Finally, start the planning process early. We've said that before, but in the family business it is for a different reason. In many succession plans, G-2, or the second generation of ownership, is about 10 to 15 years younger than the founder or senior owner. From the clients' standpoint, that isn't such a big gap to adjust to as control gradually shifts. In a family business, that age gap truly is a full generation, and the clients are your judge and jury. Suddenly working with a new owner who may be 30 years younger than they are may give your clients cause for concern. Eliminate that concern by giving them time to see your plan in action, and to work with your son or daughter (or other relation) one-on-one as a principal of the business, with you in the background.

For the best results and the widest array of planning options, advisors who want to build a family business should begin to establish a formal, written succession plan around age 50. It is likely that the process will still work later in life, but the range of solutions and the opportunities to make course corrections as the plan unfolds will be fewer and more challenging later on.

"YES, BUT . . ." (OBSTACLES TO OVERCOME)

When you put this book down and start to reflect on the choices we've outlined, we will predict two reactions (we have seen them and heard them many times before). The first will be excitement: "This is the plan I want; this *is* what I want to do and get accomplished." But your second reaction will be a cascade of "Yes, buts . . ."; that's natural and, as we mentioned, predictable, so let's tackle a few of those very real concerns before we go any further.

Obstacles in the succession planning process can be both real and imagined, but either way, as founder, they belong to you, so let's try to gain a better understanding of which category they fall into. In no particular order, here are the major issues that most founders (G-1 level owners) tell us they are most concerned about, or have a hard time reconciling, when it comes to creating an internal ownership track to support their succession plans.

Sharing the Books and Records

Most small business owners are quickly schooled in how to write off business-related expenses. These matters, and the full range of such expenses, are usually discussed only between the practice owner and his or her CPA. Sharing or disclosing this information to key employees-turned-investors, along with the founding owner's annual salary and benefit package, is often a point of significant discomfort when setting up an internal ownership plan.

The best advice is to become familiar with your state's minority shareholder laws, but don't abandon common sense. If your next-generation shareholder begins with just a 5 percent stake that you're financing in its entirety, share a copy of the annual valuation results and the basic income and expense numbers—that's enough for starters. When your next-generation shareholder(s) invest in 10 percent or more of your business, or $100,000+, they need to see what they're investing in. You would, too. This simply makes them smart investors.

Understand that there is a fair amount of restructuring that occurs at the ownership compensation level anyway, so past practices get smoothed out and the up-front use of wages and profit distribution payments will make even the highest owner's salary more palatable. Still, use this planning opportunity to steadily improve and streamline your bookkeeping practices and prepare the business for this next level. Allowing for increased business formalities is a good thing as your business grows larger and takes on more partners.

Next-Generation Personnel Who Are Not Ready, or Just Are Not Ownership Material

Of course they're not ready. Were you fully ready on day one of independent ownership? How did you know you had what it took to succeed? The challenge for next-generation advisors in an internal ownership transition is very different than for founding a business—not easier or harder, just very different.

One of the reasons that a succession plan unfolds so gradually over a series of tranches is that it gives everyone associated with the planning process time to prepare, learn, and adjust, and we'd include the client base in that list of "everyone." Use Tranche 1 as an incubator. Wait and see if your key employees or new recruits have what it takes as owners. Did they (and their spouses) make the investment when the opportunity was presented? Did they make their payments on time? Are they gradually learning to think like an owner? The answers to these questions are theoretical until the paperwork is signed and the process is committed to; then the answers become more black and white. Sit back and observe.

Investing in a small business and committing to that business for the duration of a career has a strange way of bringing about the necessary changes in behavior. Test that theory a little at a time and give yourself room to back up or change direction or simply to sell and walk away if the time comes. Remember, in Tranche 1 of most plans, you're not selling the business and your control over the cash flow; you're selling a small fragment (think 7.5 percent to 10 percent interest at most), which will revert back to you if it isn't paid for as agreed.

Let's close this section with an exclamation point. To be blunt, if the practice you've started relies on you for its future and its success, you don't own a business; you own a practice that will die at the end of your career. In the future, it will serve no one. You're going to need to help the next generation get ready, just like the previous generation helped you (hopefully). In turn, you'll be the beneficiary in terms of value, cash flow, and control. But you need to start this process before retirement looms on the horizon, or they never will meet your standards of readiness.

Next-Generation Successors Have No Money

That's true; they rarely do, at least in terms of not having significant extra funds from their compensation to invest in the business where they work. Financial strength is not the strong suit of G-2 and G-3 level ownership prospects. But what they do have is time, energy, and the ability to earn and invest lots of money from their combined wages, profits, and growing equity value over the course of their careers.

Over a 10- to 20-year plan and assuming industry average annual growth rates of 7 percent to 10 percent for independent businesses with multiple owners, the business's value and its cash flow have the capacity to double twice during the next generation's ownership path. The additional cash flow and added value can help solve or mitigate a lot of money problems over time, for them and for you.

To put this issue in perspective, over the first half of most succession plans (assuming a plan length of at least 10 years), the founding owner (G-1) is in control, does most of the work (and worrying), and makes most of the money—and still works full time, or close to it. In the second half of the plan, the next generation of owners, the succession team, gradually moves into a position of control if they have earned it, have paid for it, and have grown into leaders; they do most of the work and put in the hours, but the founding owner still makes most of the money. The successors' reward comes later, and is substantial, if all of the plan's participants work together and build on top of a solid foundation.

I'm Paying Myself with My Own Money

To be certain, there is only one source of money—the business that you started—so to some extent, you're right, at least in the initial stages; but that will change or the plan will not succeed and continue. In fairness, the wages and profits that are paid out to employees and investors are actually other people's money, and the decision of what to invest that money in is in their hands as well. Remember, they don't have to invest in your business; that is their choice.

As a general rule, most succession plans start with one simple rule: No one takes a pay cut to start the process. Over the course of a succession plan, if the practice is to grow into a business, the next-generation owner(s) will have to have adequate reason to invest their future capital (money, time, and energy) into the business you started. At some point, as the engine of production transfers to the shoulders of the succession team, they'll be paying you with their money, and doing so for a long time. You do have to help that process get started because you own the machinery.

Remember the last time you bought a house? One of those "truth in lending" disclosures had you acknowledge the actual amount of money you'll pay for your home if you make all the payments (principal plus interest) over the full length of the loan, and it was likely a very big number. The Lifestyle Succession Plan process is kind of like that, except you're the bank and you get paid that large sum of money, over time, for being patient and enabling the process to unfold. G-2 and G-3, as a team, get a 20-year "mortgage" and they share the costs of that mortgage as a team. They pay for it by working hard every day for decades to come. In exchange, they get to buy a much bigger "house" than they could otherwise afford and for a comfortable monthly payment.

This obstacle is best overcome by studying a 10- to 20-year pro forma spreadsheet and understanding how the various income streams of a small business can and should serve a business owner. The combination of wages plus profit distributions plus payments for equity, as the business continues to grow, results in most owners embracing the realities of the succession planning process.

Change

Change can be hard and very scary, and there is a lot of change when implementing a plan of succession. Restructuring your organization and compensation systems is easy on paper, but challenging to implement when others resist or counsel you to slow down and not change too much. Most advisors are quite content with a share of the revenue, and changing anyone's compensation is a natural cause for alarm.

We recommend that any change to the compensation structure not begin with a pay cut or anything that feels like a pay cut, and that includes all the owners, G-1 as well. Start the plan early, unfold it slowly, and use profit distributions instead of wages for the investment monies, and you will literally grow your way through these challenges.

Share the valuation results with your team of owners every year, but especially as they contemplate becoming owners. Let them read the logic of how and why the value of your business was determined as it was. Help them understand the value drivers of an independent financial services business. Show them the pro forma spreadsheets and what this opportunity looks like from their perspective—the obligations and the benefits, short term and long term.

Good information and lots of it, and a gentle hand tend to be the best means of overcoming past practices and preferences. We keep repeating it, but this point is important: You're not sharing or offering an investment in your business in order for G-2 and G-3 to keep getting a good paycheck. They don't need to invest and take a risk to get paid for the work they do. They're investing with the expectation of a return on that investment. Picture the company at twice its current value and cash flow, which is exactly what most pro forma spreadsheets will do with a sustained 7 percent annual top-line growth rate over the first tranche or two. Do the math and let your succession team see how that success applies to them—and then get their help in doing it. Make change a positive thing.

That said, not everyone can or should become an owner. Frankly, if your advisors receive a revenue share that is as much or more than what most owners make and they didn't have to risk a cent for it, they'd be smarter not to invest, at least if they're within 10 years of hanging it up anyway. Accept that and decide whether you should coexist and share cash flows or you should go in different directions, but always, always make such decisions as a part of a comprehensive plan that you understand and can fully articulate. That way, if you ever get lost, you can refer to your map and get back on course.

Losing Control

The obvious starting point for this discussion is our observation that 95 percent of independent advisors are one-owner practices. Suddenly having a partner, even one who owns just 10 percent of the practice, for example, is enough to send mild shock waves through many founding owners who have enjoyed complete control and total flexibility to do what they want, when they want. While the claim is a concern over loss of control, that statement usually doesn't have much to do with how much stock or ownership one has, at least not early on. If you own 90,000 voting shares and G-2 owns 10,000 voting shares, you will win every vote, every time, if it comes to a vote, and things rarely do.

The control issue tends to revolve around the fluidity and flexibility the founding owner has with the cash flow and finances. Let's face it—one of the benefits of being a sole owner is that you can pay yourself whenever you like, and, if cash flow permits, bonus yourself as the need arises. You can also run a lot of stuff through the company books (though if you're FINRA regulated, be careful with this—they really are watching!). One advisor I met told me he managed to write off his entire antique gun collection, which he proudly kept on full display in his office. On the books he labeled it under "Security System" and promised me that every gun was in firing condition if the need arose!

Yes, things will change, gradually. Again, picture your business at twice its current value and cash flows. Obviously, systems and processes will need to improve and will demand a certain level of formality and sophistication. Work with your CPA to adapt better controls over time so that, when you're a minority owner and not in full control, you can trust that your continuing share of profit distributions are by the book. But know that this discourse does not mean you cannot or should not use your small business to your advantage. You work hard, and your business needs to work hard for you, too.

A properly structured internal ownership plan should be designed to transfer control very gradually and at many levels (stock, titles, responsibilities, knowledge, authority over staff, and operations). Unlike a sale to a third party where 100 percent of the ownership and control is transferred at one time, a succession plan purposefully transfers control over many years, tranche by tranche, and then only if and when the next generation is ready. In fact, a properly structured plan extends the envelope of control well beyond the typical succession age, allowing the founding owner to remain an important part of the business well into his or her 70s or 80s if desired and appropriate.

Control is about more than just who owns the most stock or ownership interest in the business, and certainly is about more than who has the title of president or CEO. Owners who work less and less in a business but retain 100 percent ownership can quickly find that clients who learn to depend on the key staff members can create a shift in control factually if not legally. Absentee ownership does not work well or for long in a professional services business environment. A gradual transition and shared equity strategy is a much better approach for an aging generation of founding advisors.

CHAPTER 7

Succession Planning
Step-by-Step

WHERE TO START

Succession planning is not a singular event; succession is purposefully designed to unfold over the course of a career, and to be a continuing process beyond that point. Succession planning is as much a process as building a business is. Remember the definition from Chapter 1: A succession plan is a professional, written plan designed to build on top of an existing practice or business and to seamlessly and gradually transition ownership and leadership internally to the next generation of advisors. So, with all these pages behind you, where exactly do you start? Here is the definitive road map.

Start by gathering some basic but important information that will help you make informed decisions. These steps will also help your support team (CPA, attorney, succession specialists) assist you in making smart decisions based on your specific fact pattern and goals:

1. **Print out the past three years' profit-and-loss statements (P&Ls) and balance sheets.**
2. Have your practice/business formally valued.
3. Benchmark key operational data.

The last two of these steps will take about 45 to 60 days to complete, so get started as soon as possible. Remember this simple rule: quality in, quality out—you cannot obtain an accurate and useful valuation result by resorting to an online survey form. Do the job right. Completing the valuation questionnaire is going to take some work and focus, but accurately determining equity value and understanding the value drivers are very important steps in transforming your one-generational practice into an enduring business.

Your valuation results will help to assemble the numbers picture comprised of cash flow plus equity value; a succession plan, and a business, utilizes both numbers.

Understand that the valuation process is every bit as important as the valuation result. Many independent owners tell us that they learned as much about their practice or their business from completing the valuation intake form as they have done in reading about their valuation result and accompanying value drivers. FP Transitions also uses this reliable valuation data (including your P&Ls) to create your specific benchmarking results, which will compare your operational numbers to your peer group and to businesses and firms twice your size, for planning purposes.

Next, decide what it is that you want your business to do for you in the future. Don't be afraid to dream a little—it helps your support team to know what you're thinking—and then we'll figure out together what's possible. Many advisors are surprised at what is possible with a solid plan, but they don't know what to ask for. If you find yourself struggling with this step, revisit Chapter 2 and look at some of the common goals that other advisors consider important. If you're not sure what is possible, talk to your succession specialist, but don't limit yourself to what you know or what you think is possible. Gather more facts if this step isn't clear or you aren't confident and bring your support team in closer to help you.

4. Define the goals for your business and your succession plan.
5. Establish a time frame for the succession planning process.

This is the all-important point where you actually decide to start the process and when you'd like to implement the first step, usually the creation of a business partner—an investor in your business. Don't worry so much about your age or how much time you think you have left; worry instead about the value of what you've built and the clients who depend on you for making these planning decisions. We've designed succession plans for advisors well into their 70s, and, though the options and time frames might be a little more limited, there are still many great decisions and steps that they can take.

6. Design and develop your succession plan.

Every succession plan starts with general concepts, many of which have been explored in this book. These concepts are then reduced to a set of specific goals, shaped by specific numbers like revenue, expenses, growth rates, profitability, and, of course, years. These numbers are built into a pro forma spreadsheet that may look out into the future for 20 years or more—maybe not your retirement horizon, but certainly G-2's/G-3's investment horizon. Every plan is subdivided into a series of tranches that allow for periodic assessment and adjustment—actually a series of plans. Your plans are then vetted with your stakeholders (spouses, accountants, lawyers, business coaches, next-generation advisors, etc.), adjusted based on their input, and written out for consideration and possible action.

Note that implementation is not included in this step. Designing and developing a plan and implementing and documenting that plan are two separate steps, and they may be several years apart; treat them as such. First, just design and develop a plan that makes sense to you. It is okay if you end up deciding later that the plan will take too much time or energy, or that selling or merging would be easier and a better course of action. You'll be making a fully informed decision about what is best for you, your staff, and your clients. If you do decide to proceed and implement your plan, this is where the fun starts.

7. Build a foundation for success, and succession.
- Set up or adjust your entity structure.
- Adjust your organizational structure.
- Assess and adjust your compensation structure.
- Find the right advisors to support your plan.

In most cases, we're able to work with the entity you've already set up, adjusting it for ease of use (remember, we need to make it investor-friendly from a first-time owner's perspective) and for durability. If you're starting out as a sole proprietor, that's fine, too. You'll find that an entity structure, especially a flow-through entity from a tax standpoint, will add clarity to the organizational and compensation restructuring that will help transform your practice into a business.

Aside from the mechanical aspects, finding the right people is really the hard part, but you don't need to have G-2 and G-3 talent on board at the start. This is part of a plan that will be gradually implemented. More often than not, one or more current staff members step up to fill at least one of the ownership spots. Are they ready? Are you ready? Let's find out and start to work on it—Tranche 1 is called the incubator for good reason. In the event you start the process and then decide it's not for you, you're never obligated to sell more ownership.

8. Manage equity to create a bottom line.

This part isn't as hard as you might think. We find that using a series of interactive pro forma spreadsheets is a great, ongoing tool to help all owners (G-1, G-2, and G-3) find a balance between top-line compensation and bottom-line profits. As we continue to point out, the right tools for the right job are essential for advisors who want to build valuable and enduring business models. Creating a bottom line, the physical process of issuing quarterly profit distribution checks, doesn't happen overnight. It is best accomplished as part of a long-range plan, one that you'll literally grow into.

9. Create a continuity plan.

Plan on two distinct levels: First, plan as though everyone involved will live long, healthy, happy, and prosperous lives as business partners. Then separately plan for what happens if that doesn't work out. Sometimes life intervenes. Many times, if you plan well enough and work hard enough and surround yourself with good people, things have a way of turning out just fine. Either way, a continuity plan, which needs to take the form of a written continuity agreement, will help you and your team prepare for whatever comes your way.

Understand that, for a one-person, one-generational practice owner, valuation and continuity planning are steps one and two, in that order, from start to finish. In the world of a business owner, however, your best continuity solution will derive from your succession plan.

10. Tell your clients what you've done for them.

And celebrate the fact that you've taken the steps to put your business in a position that few other advisors are currently in. Use the fact that you're building a multigenerational business, not a practice built to die, to attract the best of the next-generation talent to benefit from this unique and lucrative structure.

ASSEMBLING YOUR SUPPORT TEAM

You're going to need some help in setting up your plan and supporting it over the coming years. The good news is you are not alone.

In our experience, the most valuable member of your team, once your plan makes it past the concept level, is going to be your CPA, or accountant. That's because properly managing cash flow is a daily business event, and accountants are good at this; it is what they know and do. We work comfortably with several hundred CPAs and accountants every year to assist independent advisors who are designing and implementing their plans.

Nothing in the processes discussed to this point will be unfamiliar to an experienced tax professional.

Having a good lawyer on your side is a part of the process, too. You do not necessarily need an attorney with knowledge of securities laws or even Financial Industry Regulatory Authority (FINRA) rules and regulations, but someone on your team needs to be familiar with these aspects. For the most part, find an experienced attorney who practices business law and knows a thing or two about mergers and acquisitions (M&A) work. Don't forget the important role that your attorney will perform in this process, which is to be a zealous advocate for you, and only you. Your attorney's job is to help you steer clear of risk, or at least to help you understand where the land mines are buried.

Attorneys also tend to be specialists in the documentation process—the paperwork. But draw a distinction here: Most attorneys and CPAs are not skilled in the planning phase; it is just not what they have been trained to do. To that end, don't confuse 60 pages of professionally drafted contract forms and a $20,000 legal bill with a good succession plan (a buy-sell agreement, or an operating agreement, are not succession plans by any stretch of the imagination!). If you implement the best phantom stock plan on earth and remain the only owner, your practice will die at the end of your career. You'll be one of the statistics instead of one of the business owners.

The role that we play at FP Transitions is that of a succession specialist (we prefer the term *equity manager*). We consult and coach advisors, and their broker-dealers and custodians, on the process of managing equity and the succession planning process. We bring to the table the specialized skill set of building enduring and transferable businesses in a highly regulated industry. Our backgrounds include law, taxes, securities rules and regulations, cash flow modeling, value and valuation, mergers and acquisitions, succession and continuity planning, benchmarking, and analysis—and only for this industry.

Perhaps one of the most important and unique things we offer is non-advocacy support. We are not a law firm and therefore do not represent the founder or any member of the succession team. We serve as the field marshal for the equity management/planning process and endeavor to create a formal structure and a long-range plan that will serve all constituents well for the length of their careers. We don't believe in "fighting to the finish," and we don't believe that there can be winners and losers in this process. Everyone has to work together, for a long time, and get the job done. We've been doing it this way for the past 16 years, and it has served our clients well; in hindsight, it is hard to imagine doing this work successfully any other way.

ENJOY THE PLANNING PROCESS

No two succession plans are ever the same. To that end, no single succession plan unfolds year after year without a few adjustments and tweaks. That's the nature of a plan. But that is all the more reason to plan, plan, and plan some more.

Over the course of your career, you'll hear a number of stories. One independent advisor will relate that she sold her practice for a multiple of 3.0 times gross revenue or gross dealer concession (GDC) and will offer to tell you how she did it. Another independent advisor will tell you how he granted some ownership to an ungrateful and, as it turned out, incompetent advisor who now is a full-blown competitor and that you should never do that or have a partner. Another will insist that the best practice model is the single-owner model, one over which you have total control of your income, regardless of what you do with it after you're done working—buy life insurance if you're worried about how things might end. There are always lots of stories, lots of experiences, and we suggest that you respectfully listen to each and every one.

And then go home and plan and decide for yourself what you will do, not what will happen to you. You're an independent advisor. You control your own future. To do that, you're going to need good information, a good plan, and the patience to execute it.

We made the point earlier that succession plans are kind of like a set of blueprints for your dream home. You'll need to narrow down, on your own for the most part, where and when the home will be built. But what will the home look like? What will it cost? How well will it reflect your tastes and the things you'll want to enjoy once it's built? Can you see yourself there when you're 70? How strong and durable does it need to be to withstand the elements for the next 50 years? The answers are different for everyone, and many of us learn by building, or buying and improving, more than one home. We learn from experience what we like and would like more of, and what we don't like.

Unfortunately, many advisors don't have a lot of time or patience when it comes to planning for themselves and their own businesses. That statement early in an advisor's career is intended to be an observation of the life of a busy entrepreneur; later in an advisor's career, that same statement starts to sound more like an excuse, because planning and strategizing are hard work. That, of course, is why many of your clients hire you to help them! It is so much easier to utilize the short decision chain in most practice models and hear a story, turn the boat around, and "head thataway." Don't do that.

At some point, being too busy to stop and plan ahead is a luxury you can no longer afford. Have your practice or business formally valued.

Write the equity value number down on your personal financial or wealth statement. Look at it in the context of the value of your home, your savings, your investments, and your retirement funds. Is it the largest asset you own? Is it one of the top three? Give it the proper level of priority for its place in your life. And don't forget: Unlike your other valuable assets, your work provides two levels of value: cash flow plus equity (both of which you control).

Once you've taken these steps and you know where things stand, set the dollar signs off to the side for a few minutes, because there are more important things—things to plan for. A succession plan starts with you and your dreams and goals. It's about what you want to build and what you need your business to do for you one day when you no longer jump out of bed at 6:00 A.M. in the morning and head into work with boundless energy and enthusiasm. It's going to happen, so plan for it—starting by about age 50. Embrace the changes with a realistic plan and adjust it to fit your life, not vice versa. Just don't build anymore without a clear plan for where you're going and how you are going to get there.

DOING THE MATH

This is the part that separates concept from reality, a succession idea from a formal succession plan. Does it work for all participants mathematically, after taxes? Is there sufficient cash flow? What sustainable growth rate is needed to achieve success? How long will it take to realize your value, or for G-2 and G-3 to pay off their purchase obligations? What happens to the plan when dollars are moved up to the compensation line and away from the bottom line?

At the conclusion of the planning process, those questions are turned into black-and-white answers. And well-informed decisions and plan adjustments are based on those answers and hard numbers. You become the owner of your plan.

Every succession plan should be subjected to a rigorous, comprehensive financial analysis that illustrates the long-term impact of the plan by incorporating compensation strategies and ownership changes with pro forma estimates of business growth and profitability, among other things. The analysis is tailored to each business by virtue of its valuation results (including the information gathered during the valuation process, which is why starting with a formal valuation is so critical). This is not something that can be accurately accomplished by filling in the blanks, online, in a survey approach. Doing the job right takes accurate information and analysis and planning time and experience.

Our pro forma analysis, for example, includes a series of interactive fields to help you and your succession team explore possibilities and what-if scenarios. We also provide separate viewpoints from each individual owner's position, year by year, share by share, over 5, 10, 15, or 20 years, all tied to an enormous database that provides benchmarks for similarly sized businesses. We include in the math models, if applicable, minority discounts, interest rates, payment terms, profit-based note payments, fixed note payments, and grants of stock (or ownership interests) if warranted. This is a lot to consider, but you and your team do need to consider every aspect before you start.

The point of doing the math is to lend credence to the planning concepts. Sometimes the math proves what you might have suspected—that it won't work and that you'll have to consider something else. It might be because the growth rates are too low, the overhead has crept up to too high a level over the years, or the revenue-sharing arrangements have pushed the payroll so far out of bounds that creating a bottom line is nearly impossible. But that doesn't happen too often, at least not to the point where it can't be fixed if everyone wants to make the plan work.

If you haven't done the math and tested the theories, you don't have a plan. It's as simple as that.

ESTABLISHING A FAIR PRICE

It is important that you set a fair price for what you've built, but don't turn it into a contest of wills. There is a right way and a wrong way to determine the value of your business. Understand that, in the context of supporting a succession plan, the valuation process and valuation results aren't really aimed at you anymore; as the founder, you're more of an interested bystander, so to speak! In the course of a succession plan, the valuation process and the valuation results are aimed at the next generation of advisors. They're the ones you have to impress and to teach the concept of equity, and that's why you have to learn to do it right.

The next generation of advisors, in order to embrace the unique opportunity afforded by advisors who offer an equity stake through a formal succession plan, will require a reliable method not just to determine the value of the business they are investing in, but to track the value of their investment accurately over time. The proper tool is a formal third-party valuation. This process takes some time and work, and it isn't free. As a result, some advisors prefer to just guess using a multiple of revenue, so let's address the problem using some specific numbers to frame the argument against this haphazard and unprofessional approach.

Over the past five years, the multiple paid by buyers to sellers for every dollar of recurring revenue in an independent financial services practice (fees and trails) ranged from a low of 1.47 to a high of 2.98. The multiple paid by third-party buyers for every dollar of nonrecurring revenue ranged from a low of 0.21 to a high of 1.68. That means that for the average fee-based practice or business in this industry, the range of multiples is from 0.21 to 2.98. If an authoritative source told you that the average value of a home in your area, per square foot, ranged from $21 to $298, would you feel comfortable settling for the average at $235 per square foot? You might, but even if you were, would your buyer (or group of buyers) agree to that same number without definitive proof, something more than a guess? Would you trust them as your successors if they did?

Odds are that they would prefer a much lower guess, and that's what they'll offer. In fact, your guess will invite theirs. If you don't respect the formalities of equity value derived through an authoritative process, why should your buyers?

Many advisors still have the mistaken notion that the only reasons to value their financial services business is a shareholder or partnership dispute, a marital dissolution, or at the end of a career on the eve of a complete sale of the business. Fortunately, the valuation process in this industry is rapidly advancing past this thinking as equity management gains a solid foothold. We now perform hundreds of valuations for our "shipbuilders" on an annual basis; it is no coincidence that they are building strong, valuable, and enduring businesses and attracting next-generation talent as investors. Equity management has become a part of their culture.

Establishing a fair price is one thing; consistently monitoring that value in a meaningful way to the advisor/owners is quite another. Annual valuations provide a library of valuation results, creating a historical record that is of great interest to key staff members, new partners, or recruits being offered a current or future ownership opportunity in an enduring business. Regardless of the specific valuation methodology used, it is important that the valuation process is consistently applied and cost-effective, and that the expert performing the analysis understands the unique qualities of an independent financial services business. Those qualities, or lack thereof, need to be tied to the marketplace to provide accuracy and reliability.

THE NUTS AND BOLTS OF A PLAN

There are a lot of details that must be addressed and monitored in order to make a succession plan thrive. For the most part, these are not things that you have to master, but things that you should know about.

A Multiple-Tranche Strategy

Succession planning is more like running a marathon and not at all like running a sprint. The race isn't won by the swift or the intrepid; it is won by those whose businesses are still growing 20 years from now, while they're sitting on the shores of Peter Island in the Caribbean watching the palm trees sway in the trade winds. Take that to heart. Slow the process down, and give yourself, your successors, and your clients time to adjust and benefit from the processes that are unfolding. That's how a succession plan is supposed to work.

The Lifestyle Succession Planning process sets up a pattern of gradual sales of ownership that retain the founder (G-1) in a control position until well after G-2 and G-3, the succession team, have proven themselves capable and dedicated to the task of ownership and leadership and production. Ownership is purchased (not given away) very gradually even as the business continues to increase in value over the course of years, maybe even decades. Slow and steady is the rule, provided that G-1 starts the process early enough. Regardless, the financing of the transaction works best when G-2 and G-3 have the opportunity to pay over the long term and to sign promissory notes that may be six figures long, but preferably never seven figures long; having smaller bites over a longer period of time by multiple successors tends to work best.

Most plans encompass multiple tranches or steps. Think of each tranche as a separate "watertight compartment." No matter what happens, G-1 is not obligated to sell any more stock to anyone and is not obligated to proceed to Tranche 2. G-2 and G-3, similarly, are not obligated to buy any more ownership and to invest any more of their profit distributions or take-home pay beyond the initial tranche of ownership. The idea is that everyone stands on one's own two feet and decides whether, based on the success or failure of the past tranche, to proceed and do it again.

Of course, having a group of successors (i.e., the succession team) tilts the advantage slightly in G-1's favor, but only slightly, and, in fairness, it offsets the risk of selling internally to one or more successors who typically don't have any money (or at least not a spare hundred thousand dollars or two). This gradual process, enhanced by the use of drag-along and tag-along rights in the buy-sell agreement, tends to keep everyone motivated and focused on the task at hand and in moving forward with all due speed.

One last point worth mentioning is that, although the Lifestyle Succession Planning process moves forward in a series of tranches, it isn't like a 16-year-old driver letting out the clutch for the first time. The process tends to unfold more smoothly when everyone is working at the process. When it works to everyone's satisfaction, it is not at all unusual to roll up Tranche

1 into Tranche 2 and accelerate the process. Conversely, even when, maybe especially when Tranche 1 works faster and better than anyone could have imagined, G-1 has the ability and the power to slow things down and take a year or two off between each tranche before proceeding.

People who think succession planning is about losing control really have no idea how the process works.

It Is All about Growth

Every morning in Africa, a gazelle wakes up. It knows it must run faster than the fastest lion or it will be killed. Every morning a lion wakes up. It knows it must outrun the slowest gazelle or it will starve to death. It doesn't matter whether you are a lion or a gazelle. When the sun comes up, you'd better start running!

(African proverb)

How do you get the next-generation talent pool to accept and embrace the fact that buying stock or ownership gradually in a growing business (i.e., a business they're helping to grow) means that each subsequent purchase will be more expensive than the last? The answer is, turn that into good news by connecting those growth rates to both their take-home pay and their ability to buy more stock faster. Here's how it can work as part of a comprehensive succession plan.

Independent financial services and advisory practices have a decided advantage when it comes to attracting and retaining next-generation talent: strong, sustainable growth fueled by recurring income sources and predictable overhead structures. Last year, FP Transitions' Research and Analytics department conducted a study on growth rates, titled "Independent Financial Service Growth Rate Study." Following is an excerpt from this study, along with an illustrative chart (Figure 7.1).

The macroeconomic exposure of financial services practices to positive growth factors is unique when compared against other mature industries in the United States. Consider this: If an advisor simply maintains his or her client base, and we assume an average market portfolio for every client under management, then the assets under management for that advisor will grow at approximately the rate of market growth, before distributions. According to the Federal Reserve, the average annual return on stocks, Treasury bills, and Treasury bonds for the period from 1962 to 2011 was 10.60 percent, 5.22 percent, and 7.24 percent, respectively (including dividend returns

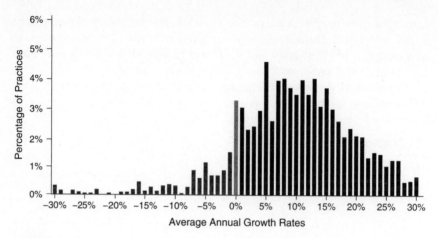

FIGURE 7.1   Growth Rates of Financial Practices from 2002 to 2011

and coupons on fixed income securities). For the period 2002–2011, the market returns were 4.93 percent, 5.22 percent, and 7.24 percent for stocks, Treasury bills, and Treasury bonds, respectively.

Our analysis, computed from information we collect directly from our clients, suggests that revenue growth over the 2002–2011 period was 13 percent, with the middle 50 percent of the distribution growing by between 5 percent and 16 percent annually. Our data for this particular study included practices that ranged in size from $1 million in assets under advisory/management up to $2 billion in assets. There was no statistical significance when controlled for the size of the underlying practice, business, or firm, meaning that the largest practices grew at the same rate as the smallest practices, on average.

Clearly this is a positive reflection on the financial services industry as a whole—advisors are not simply limited to the long-term growth of the markets. Independent advisors can add assets and clients to their practices, increase death benefits as part of the planning process, and create a multigenerational asset platform to defray the negative revenue effect of clients and assets that are in the distribution phase of their life cycle.

In a typical succession plan, the next generation builds on top of an established business and, as a team of owners, they work together to build a stronger and deeper organization. The reward is illustrated both in the improving multiple of gross revenue or earnings and in the total realized equity value by the founder. The final results tend toward a value, expressed as a multiple of gross revenue, of about six times the starting point, not including a reasonable salary for the owner for the duration. In addition, founders benefit from a reduced workload in the second half of the plan and a built-in continuity plan to protect business value as the practice is transformed into a multigenerational business.

The presence of one or more internal successors is intended to support and accelerate growth even as the founding owner gradually retires on the job. This is in stark contrast to the single-owner model where production tends to decline rapidly as the founding owner works less and less as the founder nears retirement. Growth is imperative if you're building something that can outlive you. You cannot attract next-generation talent to support your model if you aren't growing. The ship either is under power or it is adrift.

Finally, never lose sight of one simple fact: Growth is the reason next-generation advisors invest their money, time, and careers into the process of building an enduring business, and building on top of your existing practice model. Growth provides the return on investment and the means by which ownership is paid for. Succession planning is all about sustainable, long-term growth, and that is why this is one of the steps you need to understand and build around on the path forward.

Proper Application of Minority Discounts

Minority and marketability discounts are adjustments to the fair market value of stock because the minority interest owner(s) cannot direct or control the business operations and because the minority interest lacks marketability. G-2 and G-3 owners will invariably become minority owners. In fact, it is highly likely that, by Tranche 3, your business may never again have a single, majority shareholder. This is part of the shift from the "strong man" approach where one person does it all to the collaborative environment where no one person can excel unless the business as a whole does well.

Understand that as a business owner, it is entirely your decision whether to offer a minority discount. If you do offer a discount, it is also acceptable to never, ever offer another one regardless of whether your next-generation staff members are purchasing another minority ownership interest. If you're an S corporation, mind that "one class of stock" rule and be consistent in applying discounts from one shareholder to the next. Most of the succession plans we set up employ only one minority discount, that in Tranche 1, and then never again.

A minority interest is noncontrolling ownership, usually defined as less than 50 percent of a company's voting shares. A minority discount, at least in the case of an amicable buy-in situation, is a reduction in the price of stock from its fair market value because the minority interest owner(s) cannot direct or control the business operations, and because of lack of marketability and therefore liquidity of the shares.

A minority discount applied to a noncontrolling ownership interest in a small business reflects the notion that a partial ownership interest may be worth less than its pro rata (proportional) share of the total business. For example, ownership of a 25 percent share in the business may be worth less than 25 percent of the entire business's value. This is so because this 25 percent ownership share may be limited as to control over critical aspects of the business, including:

- Electing the company's directors and appointing its officers
- Declaring and distributing profits (dividends or profit distributions)
- Entering into contractual relationships with customers and suppliers
- Raising debt or equity capital
- Hiring and dismissing employees or officers
- Selling the business or acquiring other operations

In practical terms, the applicable range of discounts is generally between 10 percent and 40 percent, though it is imperative that every owner and investor confer with his or her CPA/accountant as to what is reasonable and appropriate in each situation. The amount of the minority discount is not set or specifically established by law. It depends on a number of factors and is adjusted for any given situation, rather than being applied as a universal standard. Note that it is appropriate to calculate separate discounts for lack of control and lack of marketability, but the cumulative total should be within the range of 10 percent to 40 percent (see Figure 7.2). A discount, if offered, should be applied fairly and evenly. For example, if a 10 percent interest in the business is being sold to two members of a succession team at or at about the same time, the same valuation method and the same level of discounting (if any) should apply to each sale.

That said, here's the practical side of this argument. Consider that in most internal sales of independent financial services and advisory businesses,

MARKET VALUE

MINORITY DISCOUNT 10% to 40%	PURCHASE PRICE LACK OF CONTROL, LIQUIDITY, AND MARKETABILITY

FIGURE 7.2   Application of Minority Discounts to Sale of Stock

the owner or seller of the stock (G-1) almost always provides very generous financing terms enabling the purchase of the minority shares, perhaps
even providing the funding through profit distributions or a salary increase or
bonus. Also consider that, in the majority of cases we work with, the minority
owners have a direct path to majority ownership upon the founding owner's
death, disability, or retirement, usually through a written continuity or succession plan (i.e., a buy-sell or shareholders' agreement), which also, again, is
usually accompanied by very generous, long-term financing from the founding owner or the business itself. More succinctly, the buyers rarely pay cash or
even a significant down payment for the ownership interest they've acquired
or are about to acquire. The seller has to wait, be patient, and take the risk,
usually without a corresponding interest rate to reflect that position.

For all these reasons, many owners choose not to provide any minority
discount or, if they do, it is offered only on purchases in Tranche 1 of the
succession planning process to help get the process started. All subsequent
purchases of stock, regardless of the minority position of the buyer, are at
fair market value as determined by a formal valuation within six months of
the date of the transaction.

Granting of Ownership

It bears repeating: Don't give away your business. This isn't just a philo-
sophical issue; the IRS is waiting in the wings for its fair share of every
stock grant you choose to issue. Equity compensation is a powerful growth
strategy, but it often has debilitating tax consequences. Let's dive into the
mechanics of this process, sort it out, and figure out how to make this strategy work for you if grants are your preference.

Granting of stock or ownership creates obligations and tax issues. Obligations first: If the recipient of the grant doesn't stay and work for you forever, you're going to have to buy that stock back (be very careful if you're an
S corporation, as treating the granted stock differently or placing a separate
or nominal value on it for buy-back purposes can violate the "one class of
stock" rule and cause you to revert to C corporation status). The best way
to control this issue is with a shareholders' agreement or other form of
buy-sell agreement. The flip side of this is that if something happens to you
as the founder and, for example, the 98 percent owner of the business, the
2 percent owner by way of a grant is now the surviving shareholder. Is this
shareholder ready for what comes next? That's why granting stock has to
be part of a comprehensive plan and why we recommend selling stock first,
granting it only to augment the purchase.

Section 102(a) of the Internal Revenue Code provides the rule that gifts
are not subject to federal income tax. However, Section 102(c) provides that

gifts from an employer to an employee are fully taxable to the employee as ordinary income. Not only are such gifts, which certainly include stock, subject to state and federal income tax, but they are treated as employee compensation to be reported on Form W-2—meaning that the employer must pay and withhold employment taxes on the value of the ownership interest gifted to the employee. For this reason, stock or ownership grants are often referred to as "equity compensation."

This result is due in part to a U.S. Supreme Court case, *Commissioner v. Duberstein.* In that case, the Court defined a gift, for federal tax purposes, as a transfer of property made out of the donor's "detached and disinterested generosity." In most situations, the IRS finds that a gratuitous transfer of property made in the context of a business relationship is neither "detached" nor "disinterested." On the contrary, a majority owner is often intensely involved and interested in the effect that a new owner has upon the business, especially for succession planning purposes. Such a "gift" is taxed to the recipient as ordinary income.

Taxation on the transference of shares or an ownership interest can be complicated, and the advice of a CPA or tax attorney should be sought in every instance involving the purchase, sale, or granting of stock in a business. However, the following rules can generally be applied:

- *Fair market value/basis.* The taxable fair market value of shares transferred to employees (such as through equity compensation or a stock grant) is the value of the stock, less any amount paid by the employees from their own funds for the shares—and this amount becomes the recipient's basis in the stock.
- *Company withholding/deductibility.* The company can deduct the taxable value of the shares given as a benefit of employment in the year that employees claim the value of shares received as part of their income for tax purposes. While this substantially shifts the tax burden to the employee, the employer is still responsible for the payment of payroll taxes on the value transferred.
- *Vesting issues.* If the granted shares are restricted shares and the restrictions create a "significant risk of forfeiture" because the conditions may not be met, then the employees have a choice about taxes: either pay taxes in that year or wait and pay taxes in the year when the transfer restrictions expire. They can file an 83(b) election (within 30 days of receiving the stock) and choose to pay ordinary income tax on the value of the shares (their fair market value minus any amount paid for them) at the time of the grant. No additional tax is owed until those shares are sold and then the owner of those shares will pay capital gains tax on the difference between the value declared for the 83(b) election and

the sale price. If the employee fails to meet the conditions, however, and receives no shares (i.e., the shares are eventually forfeited), the tax paid cannot be recaptured. If the employee does not file this election, then when the shares are received (not sold), the employee pays ordinary income tax on their current fair market value minus any consideration paid for them.

Because a vesting schedule can interfere with the shareholder's ability to receive profit distributions, most succession planning strategies utilized by independent financial services owners do not rely on this strategy for tax mitigation purposes. Instead, stock grants are more commonly used to augment a key employee's purchase of stock, serving as reward and motivation for the extended tenure required to pay for ownership out of profit distributions and future growth on an after-tax basis. In other words, buying stock internally by next-generation talent takes a long time. Stock grants, within the context of a formal succession plan, provide an incentive to stay put, and serve to accelerate the purchase when using profit distributions as the primary method of repayment.

So here is how to use grants strategically. If the goal is to sell 20 percent of your ownership in Tranche 1, or 20,000 shares or units to two advisors (G-2) cumulatively, start by selling less than that amount, say 7,500 shares or units per buyer. Use a profit-based note that ties their payments to their receipt of profit distribution checks (which G-1 controls in amount and timing). Don't require that G-2 use all of their profit distributions (after taxes) toward principal and interest on the note; instead, let them take home part of those profits—an important step in connecting the bottom line to take-home pay. Compel G-2 to pay in somewhere around 50 percent or more of their after-tax profit distributions, and leave it to them to invest more. Sit back and observe, but provide them some incentive and reward to do better and go faster (and to help the company grow more profitably). Here's one way to do it.

As G-2 pays off every 20 percent to 25 percent of their profit-based note, have the company grant them additional shares or units with the goal of reaching 10 percent ownership (after dilution) by the end of Tranche 1. The catch is that G-2 has to stay on board for the duration; there are stiff penalties usually imposed if they leave early for any bad reason or reason detrimental to the interests of the business and its succession plan (e.g., quit, set up a competing practice, get fired, etc.).

Stock grants or equity compensation, used in such a manner, helps to solve the tenure issue, which means this is a long-term, career-length investment. How do you get a 30-year-old, first-time business owner to commit to a 20- to 30-year process? Our experience to date and our best guess is that if G-2 stays for the duration of Tranche 1, they'll stay for the duration. By that time, this investment will be for them what it is for you: the largest, most valuable investment they own.

The combination of a purchase price at fair market value less an appropriate minority discount, with no pay cut, no significant down payment, a return on investment of 7 percent to 10 percent annually that comes with a paycheck and a mentor, certainly makes this the best investment opportunity they will likely ever have access to. In this industry, smart investors recognize and embrace smart investments, especially those over which they exert a significant amount of control.

Shareholder Dilution and Oppression Issues

This is the part where many owners gulp and say, "I knew this was going to get complicated." Maybe, maybe not, but owning a business has never been for the faint of heart, so swallow hard and let's move through this section. Shining a bright light on these issues, and understanding them, often provides a level of comfort and control. You just have to know these things are out there.

Because of the gradual transfer of business equity that occurs during the course of most succession plans in the financial services industry, next-generation owners (G-2 or G-3) initially hold a minority ownership interest in the business (i.e., an ownership interest in less than 50 percent of the corporate stock or LLC membership units). No surprise—owners in a minority position are usually subject to the will of the majority owner when it comes to the management of the business. That is commonplace and to be expected. However, the majority owner may go a step further and aggressively use his or her power against the minority owner, and that can be a problem.

For example, the majority owner may vote against the company's payment of a dividend or distribution and thereby deprive the minority owner of the company's profits, or deny the minority owner access to company books and records. The majority owner might take all of the growth and channel those monies through his or her own paycheck as a bonus, leaving nothing in the new and modernized compensation structure for G-2 and G-3 level ownership. Those examples may be considered instances of shareholder oppression, which occurs when the majority owner exercises his or her power in a way that exploits or intentionally harms the minority owner.

We commonly warn all succession planning participants (G-1, G-2, and G-3) about this issue, however, because both the senior advisor(s) and junior advisors may well become minority owners at some point during the succession planning process. In fact, plan on it. In the most common scenario,

G-2 and G-3 level advisors are minority owners from the beginning of the succession plan to at least the middle of the plan (and maybe for the duration), and the G-1 advisor may become a minority owner from the middle of the plan to the end.

Shareholder oppression can pose a serious threat to minority owners of closely held businesses. Unlike publicly traded companies, in closely held businesses minority owners do not have a market in which they can liquidate their interests. If the minority owner is able to find a buyer, the sale price for the minority interest is usually subject to a large discount, but for the most part, such options are foreclosed by the buy-sell agreement. These factors can make the minority owners of a closely held business feel trapped if they find themselves in an oppressive situation. Worse, it may prevent them from investing altogether, and instead they become a competitor.

These issues may seem troubling, but the good news is that both the law and skillful planning can usually resolve them. While the law has provisions to protect business owners who hold minority interests, a lawsuit is the absolute last resort; it remains important to acknowledge its possibility, however, and then to implement a better strategy of protection through adept planning and fair dealing.

When G-1, G-2, and G-3 advisors address the issues of shareholder dilution that may arise as part of a succession plan, it is important that they remain focused on the big picture. Shareholder dilution, in and of itself, may not necessarily be a bad thing—especially in the context of a growing business. For example, an existing shareholder may balk at learning that his or her ownership percentage will be reduced from 10 percent to 8 percent following the admission of a new shareholder. But what would the response be if, as a result of that transaction, the value of the business were to increase from $1,000,000 to $1,500,000? In terms of dollar value, 8 percent of $1,500,000 ($120,000) is worth more than 10 percent of $1,000,000 ($100,000).

Advisors who have zero tolerance for shareholder dilution can prevent it with the use of an antidilution agreement. There are generally two types of antidilution agreements or provisions: full-ratchet and weighted-average. A full-ratchet agreement increases an owner's interest to the amount he or she would have owned at the lower offering price paid by incoming buyers, regardless of how much the original owner owns or how little the incoming buyers purchase. Alternatively, a weighted-average agreement uses a formula that takes into account the quantity of stock sold at the lower offering price. Both options should be discussed and reviewed with legal counsel and tax counsel before negotiation and implementation.

An effective way to inhibit shareholder oppression is to draft into the enterprise agreement a buyout clause that defines and is triggered by the majority owner's oppressive conduct against the minority owner. The clause would obligate the majority owner to purchase the minority owner's interest at a defined value if triggered. The value should ideally be tied to an authoritative, neutral, and market-based valuation of the business at the time when the minority owner invokes the clause. Such a clause not only gives the minority owner an economic remedy against shareholder oppression, but it can also deter shareholder oppression by putting the majority owner on guard against the obligation of purchasing the minority owner's interest at a price favorable to the minority owner—a demand that the majority owner may be unwilling or unable to meet. FP Transitions' standard enterprise agreements can include this form of protection.

DOCUMENTATION

To recap, the succession planning process typically involves two distinct phases. Phase one focuses on design and development of your custom plan. Phase two is about documentation and implementation of your plan—in other words, the paperwork necessary to make your plan a reality. The paperwork and contracts necessary to support succession plans may include the following:

- Multiple stock purchase agreements (one for each advisor/successor)
- Promissory notes (fixed or profit-based format)
- Amortization schedules (in advance for a fixed note, in arrears for a profit-based note)
- Stock grants
- Stock pledges (collateralization)
- Employment agreements
- Corporate resolutions/recapitalization events
- Shareholders' or buy-sell agreements
- Operating agreements (for corporate tax structures)

In about 20 percent of the plans, the process commences with the selection and setting up of an entity structure. Since this step often builds in a delay of one year in order for G-1 to obtain long-term capital gains tax treatment on the sale of his or her stock in Tranche 1, it is important to consider this aspect as part of the anticipated implementation time frame. For everyone else, the process commences with a recapitalization event to reset the existing structure and prepare it for the duration and plan specifics.

All documentation, once prepared on a plan-specific basis, should be reviewed by local legal counsel for each participant. In most cases, the documents are virtually identical as to each member of the succession team, which helps to create a fair and level playing field and allows the process to proceed at a fairly brisk pace. The tax issues for the plan are typically reviewed during the plan design and development phase and then carried over into the documentation.

Promissory notes in Tranche 1 are generally nonrecourse and tend to be profit-based as opposed to fixed notes. As a result, the buy-sell protocol (i.e., the continuity agreement) restricts the rights of investors who leave the plan for any reason other than death or disability prior to completion of the first tranche, but these items are always negotiable within reason.

Separate documents are executed at each tranche. Most plans are accompanied by formal, annual valuations of the business, part of our basic Equity Management System (EMS) or the enhanced Succession Maintenance Program (SMP). G-2 and G-3 level owners are encouraged to review and approve the valuation inputs and are provided a copy of the valuation results. Stock should be sold and purchased (or, on occasion, granted) at fair market value, so the ability to monitor and determine that value annually is an important aspect to the succession planning process.

Limited liability companies (LLCs) may require an amendment of the operating agreement, depending on the plan, which may need to include a unit structure and other corporate attributes to create some level of rigidity and predictability in the entity structure and operational format—it matters to minority owners. LLCs taxed as partnerships will need to rely on local legal counsel to custom draft the agreement based on the specifics of the actual plan. Other than for this element, local legal counsel tends to review and augment a set document package designed to address the specific plan elements and goals.

BANK FINANCING—EXPANDING YOUR OPTIONS

Whether you're considering selling your business externally to the best-qualified buyer or internally to a team of successors, bank financing solutions can provide powerful tools to reshape or to accelerate your plans (see Figure 7.3).

Bank financing solutions for independent financial professionals looking to buy or sell a financial services practice have been almost nonexistent in years past. That has changed. Today, qualified banks are now lending to next-generation advisor/owners who have a formal succession plan. As a result, lending and funding solutions now can provide a retiring owner with the ability to quickly cash out of the business if that business has the necessary foundations and personnel in place. In other words, founding owners can decide exactly when, over the course of a 10- to 20-year plan, they'd like

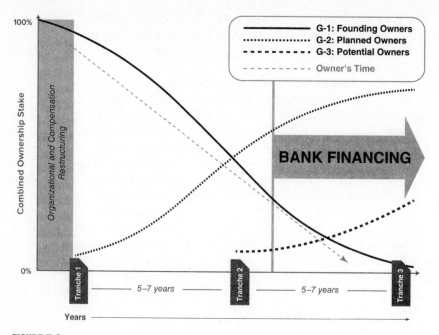

FIGURE 7.3 Succession Planning with Bank Financing

to step away from the business in favor of a team of internal successors who have proven themselves capable on the job.

Since the year 1999 when FP Transitions first launched and subsequently orchestrated the open market concept for independent practice owners, the rule in almost every transaction has been that of seller financing. Strong, well-positioned buyers (not usually consolidators) came in, paid a substantial down payment (30 percent to 40 percent) out of cash reserves, and then dedicated the acquired cash flow to paying the balance in three to six years with at least one contingency to ensure a motivated seller. The result was a shared-risk/shared-reward transaction, and it worked well, whether the buyer was a third party or an employee, son, or daughter.

Seller financing has certainly proven its value; the shared-risk/shared-reward concept between buyer and seller has routinely delivered 90 percent to 100 percent client transition and retention rates in the years following the sale of the practice—often to a complete stranger from the clients' perspective. But the benefits have also had a cost; seller financing placed two-thirds of the risk of every transaction on the shoulders of the seller, while immediately transferring full control of the cash flow to the buyer. In addition, sellers have had to play the role of banker and wait years to fully realize the value they'd built over a lifetime. Occasionally, the financing period was interrupted by events beyond anyone's control—think recession, market fluctuations, regulatory issues, and the like.

The ability to professionally finance an independent financial services transaction, internal or external, provides a powerful new tool when used correctly and as part of a well-constructed plan designed to maximize client retention and tax benefits. Bank financing provides a business founder with the option of either seller-financing the entire transaction over the span of a decade or two (with the attendant benefits in terms of value and cash flow and control or participation) or opting out of the lengthy process at a time of his or her choosing, eliminating the lending risk, and leaving the proven and committed succession team to work with a qualified lender.

Given that more than a few of today's founding owners are starting the succession planning process five to 10 years late, bank financing has become an important consideration and is typically built into every plan, just in case. One of the reasons succession plans are successful is because they don't lock in positions or obligations too far into the future. A sound plan must provide its participants with room to adapt because, inevitably, there will be course corrections.

BEWARE OF BENCHMARKS AND SURVEY RESULTS

Go back to square one: *99 percent of today's independent financial services and advisory practices will not survive the founder's retirement or the end of the founder's individual career. When the advisor leaves, for whatever reason, it's over.* So what do you think will happen if you pattern your business decisions on data and survey results from a group of fellow owners who are heading over the cliff? Do you really want to follow a model and a stream of data from practices built to die? Do you think your results will be any different if you use benchmarks from hundreds of one-generational practice models? Lots and lots of bad data doesn't start to make it good data. This isn't about feeling right; this process is about getting it right.

If you're going to use benchmarks as guideposts on your journey, be sure you're getting good data; specifically, you need to benchmark against businesses and firms, not practices designed for just one generation. Benchmark your business against other shipbuilders, not the life rafts or the flotillas. There is a lot of data available to you in the independent financial services industry. Before you rely on any of it, ask yourself these simple questions:

- What are your goals for the future? What do you want to build? Is it a valuable and enduring business?

- Who supplied the information you're thinking of relying on—one-owner practices or multigenerational businesses? Are the data reflective of practices below where you're at, on par, or businesses twice your size?
- Is the practice data useful in building an enduring and valuable business model?
- Have the owners of these practices or businesses ever accomplished what you are setting out to do?
- If you do exactly what the crowd did that supplied the data, where will you likely end up?

I had the recent opportunity to talk to an independent advisor who wrote a great article on building an enduring business model and setting up an internal ownership track. He championed next-generation talent and their role in helping practice owners build enduring businesses. I was taken aback when, in asking him about his own business structure, I learned that he actually was not an owner of the business, which was rather a siloed model that had clear and strong fracture lines built into the foundation— deliberately built into the one-generational practice. This was an advisor who wanted to be part of a business, but who accepted a revenue-sharing arrangement and the opportunity to build an individual book because "that's how it's done in this industry."

Too much of this industry follows that pattern. It is time to change direction and take control. Build your own team and create your own future.

CHAPTER 8

A Tale of Ownership

Everyone who creates a succession plan will explore and find one's own path, but that doesn't mean that you can't learn from others who have gone before you. This is the first generation of independent owners who have had to grapple with the fact that their practices, sometimes businesses, have amassed significant value. It's only natural that, at this point, there will be more questions than answers. How best to handle a succession plan when you're unsure of the path, unsure of the next-generation talent base? When is it too soon to start worrying, or too late to start planning? Where does one get good, reliable advice? What if things go wrong, or don't go as planned? If any of those concerns sound familiar, this story is for you.

SUCCESSION PLANNING CASE STUDY

James Warren operated Strategic Financial Management from a beautifully refurbished turn-of-the-century home in South Bend, Indiana. He had a staff of seven, four of whom were qualified advisor/producers in this hybrid, fee-based model. The four advisors, one of whom was James's daughter, ranged in age from 27 to 38, and most had or were completing their Certified Financial Planner (CFP) course work; one had a Chartered Financial Analyst (CFA) designation as well.

Over the course of 30 years of work, James had gained a lot of experience, starting with a wirehouse, then moving to an insurance-based broker-dealer, then to a predominantly fee-based independent model under his stand-alone Registered Investment Adviser (RIA) while maintaining a relationship with an independent broker-dealer. As the years passed and James moved into his late 50s, he began to think seriously about his own succession plans and how he could better utilize and rely on the talents of his next-generation advisors to build an enduring and transferable business. James was working, on average, only about 30 hours a week at this point, and he had a comfortable living from a stable practice with predictable cash flow.

James had done most things right. He had set up an S corporation about 10 years earlier of which he was the 100 percent owner. He'd had his practice formally valued for the first time about five years ago; the valuation opinion of $2.1 million in 2008 was satisfying, but still a bit short of the mark based on James's retirement goals.

James dutifully attended all of the succession planning presentations and webinars he could find, and he read the many magazine articles on this subject. So, when he first sat down with his company's legal and tax counsel to discuss the issue of his own succession plan, he felt like he had a solid grasp of the subject matter. However, his lessons were just beginning.

James's attorney strongly advised him to retain ownership of all of the stock in his S corporation and full, 100 percent control of his business until the day when he was ready to walk away—and then to sell the business to his key employees and next-generation advisors if they could come up with the money or a solid repayment plan. James pushed back and said that he didn't have a clear exit point in his career, but that he was certain that such a date was at least seven or eight years in the future. He also expressed the concern that his key staff members might not be patient enough and still willing to work there and help him add another million dollars of value to the business if no ownership opportunity was forthcoming along the way.

The law firm suggested that James create a phantom stock plan to create "ownership-like benefits" in the meantime; that way, the key staff members could be rewarded monetarily for helping grow and strengthen the business. James's attorney did his job well and shared a horror story or two with James about what it is like to have a bad partner, or to have to buy out a partner who subsequently leaves with part of the client base. James's CPA was consulted as well, and after no objections were raised, several drafts of the plan were drawn up, reviewed, and ultimately presented to James's key staff members.

The plan was discussed and analyzed in depth by James and his team over the course of the next year, and ultimately, $25,000 in legal and tax consulting fees later, all of the licensed producers rejected it, preferring instead to have a real ownership opportunity; they wanted to own stock in the business where they worked and to begin to amass an ownership position in the growing business and become principals of the business—just like James.

The advisors argued that a phantom stock plan would certainly provide them with additional compensation, for which they were grateful, but would not put them in a good position to buy out James's ownership upon his retirement, or earlier in the event of his sudden disability or death. And then there was the nagging problem of buying what they felt they were building and already owned in some sense of the word.

The advisors were also concerned that James was beginning to reduce his hours worked and that more and more of the workload and the responsibility for growth were falling on their shoulders, with no ownership stake and no commensurate reward for the added workload. James told his team that he'd like to reduce his hours worked by another full day over the coming years as he got older, giving them more and more opportunity to make decisions and become leaders of the business, along with annual pay raises and bonuses to compensate them. But the harder they worked, they argued, the further the succession team was from buying out James's position. In the end, buying out a growing company from a zero ownership position while James maintained his full salary and benefits felt a little disingenuous to them.

After another year or so passed, James decided to try something different. He hired a professional consulting company to help him—an investment banker familiar with the independent financial services sector. This second firm wisely counseled him on the merits of an internal ownership track and the benefits to James and his team by transitioning ownership internally, over time. They conducted a valuation of James's firm, and did a thorough operational review. In the end, it all came down to one big question: Did James's key staff members—his four potential investors—have what it would take to buy and run the business?

To answer that question, the consulting firm proposed putting the key staff members through a series of interviews and tests to try to determine if these next-generation advisors had what it would take to become owners and entrepreneurs. The process was thorough, even arduous. And in the end, the answer was, sadly, "No." While the individuals ranked at various points along the evaluation spectrum, some being potential prospects with limited upside and others being rejected out of hand, the decision was made that selling internally was not a viable option. The investment banker's expert opinion was to wait until James was ready to fully retire and walk away, and then sell the firm externally for several million dollars. They would, of course, be pleased to handle the sales process.

There was just one problem: James's next-generation staff members still wanted to buy him out and were quite insistent that they would prove they had what it takes—on the job. So, after another year or so, James tried a third approach. He hired one more consultant and had the company revalued; this was an issue because the next-generation advisors did not fully trust the valuation processes they were seeing, and, as potential investors, they cared a lot about the value of the business. This time, James let two of his key staff members participate in the valuation input process, even reviewing the company's income statements (for the first time) and providing the financial data, client demographic data, overhead and cost structures, compensation levels, and profitability during the valuation process.

Once the valuation was complete, the results were shared with the four advisors, and while the number was even larger than before, it was better received; this was a valuable fee-based business with good client demographics. The consultant developed and designed a detailed plan with James's and his advisors' input that allowed for a very limited initial buy-in to field-test the plan and observe how it worked. In the end, would this investment be as important to James's next-generation team as it was to James and his wife, the founders of the company? Time would tell.

The investors would cumulatively purchase 20 percent of James's stock, signing long-term, profit-based promissory notes (see Chapter 6 for more information on the Lifestyle Succession Plan). While the plan didn't rely on anyone taking a cut in pay to make the investment, it did rely on a strong and sustainable growth rate, responsibility for which was to gradually transfer from James to the succession team. The investors, as James took to calling them, would have to prove to James and to themselves that they could eventually prosper on their own without his help—with the money coming from a redesigned cash flow structure capable of paying James many times more than the rules of thumb he'd heard about.

One of the most difficult parts of the plan was rethinking and restructuring the compensation strategy at the ownership level. James and his team had always been paid primarily based on what they produced—a revenue-sharing arrangement. As business owners, James realized that his succession team could no longer afford to focus on just one aspect of the business, even one as important as cash flow; there were too many other things they'd have to learn to do and be motivated to succeed at. The succession team would need to learn to work together and to widen their focus even while maintaining production of revenue as job number one. Somehow, the duties of maintaining or even improving profitability and all the systems and processes needed to continue to grow a strong and enduring business model had to enter the picture.

To help the succession team learn to work and think from an owner's perspective, their consultant advised on shifting to a profit-based business model, essentially using the S corporation's cash flow structure to do what it was designed to do: create business owners who are paid a reasonable wage for their work and a profit distribution in return for their investment. The profit-based business approach maintained revenue generation as the starting point, but used the payment of profit distributions (limited to actual owners) to connect the cost of that growth to each owner's paycheck. On paper, it was clean and looked so easy to do.

But for the advisors, letting go of their revenue-sharing arrangements proved a challenge; instead of relying primarily on their own efforts to earn their paychecks and building their own books, the investors would now need to learn to work more as a team, a succession team, and to build one strong enterprise instead of four or five individual books. Revenue sharing was how they'd always done it, it was all they knew, and it was what they had been taught was normal. James, on the other hand, now in his early 60's, wasn't working as hard as he used to; his production was dropping. He was fully supportive of the plan, and acknowledged that he wished he had made the switch from a revenue-sharing model to a profit-based business 10 years earlier!

Two key steps helped the team work past this critical issue: (1) the promise that the investment opportunity would not require a pay cut to any of the investors and (2) the realization that, as owners, they would have two ways to earn their money from now on—wages plus profits—one tied to their individual efforts, the other result of the team's collective effort. The consultant provided detailed spreadsheet models of the restructured cash flow model projections and showed the succession team the possible results 10 to 15 years into the future using conservative growth rates tied to the business's actual cost structure. The advisors studied the data, did their homework, and did a lot of thinking, and then announced that they were ready to invest—all of them.

The plan was launched. Shortly after James's 63rd birthday, he proudly announced in the company newsletter and a press release to the community newspaper that his business had expanded and now welcomed four new principals to better serve multiple generations of clients. Shortly thereafter, James further reduced his time in the office to an average of about two days a week, probably a little too soon, but there were other things he wanted to do. And he still watched over everything very carefully and checked in by phone on a daily basis. The succession team began to sort things out among themselves with James always available as a mentor and guide. James continued to meet with the largest and longest-tenured clients, and put a positive spin on the transition within his growing and enduring business.

The next-generation advisors were running more and more of the operations on their own, gradually proving the business could survive without James, at least in terms of client servicing. Eighty percent of the clients now had not met with James one-on-one in the past three or more years anyway, and the team seemed more than up to the job. Unfortunately, that wasn't enough. As a new and younger group of advisors, the succession team faced challenges James had never been exposed to.

When James started the business some 30 years before, he quite literally began from scratch. He didn't borrow any money, unless you count the credit card bills and the rising personal debt that resulted from a lack of paychecks. He still had the first dollar he'd ever earned in a frame behind his desk, along with other mementos and awards he'd earned over the years, and there were many. Back then, James made all the decisions and did most of the work—he was the "engine of production"; he made everything go. There wasn't much input from others, but the decision-making chain was short and efficient!

For James's team of advisors, it was very different. The consultant advised James to begin the process either with equal ownership for the entire team or by forming two levels based on age or experience (or both) and providing equal ownership opportunities to each separate team or level. This approach was intended to balance the investment opportunity at the start of the process and, rather than anointing any one person to be the leader, to rely on the team of successors to figure that out on their own, certainly with James's help and input as their mentor.

But the advisors didn't all get along so well. The oldest and most experienced advisor, the CFA, also had more financial strength, and he made his payments on the note much faster than everyone else could. He had a different problem in that he could not effectively command the others. As a new owner, he changed, becoming more demanding of himself and everyone around him, to the point of divisiveness. One year later, he was gone, dismissed by James with the support of the entire office (yes, owners can still be fired, and this guy was). The business was solid and still growing, and the remaining three next-generation owners, who had matured beyond their years, stepped it up a notch and worked through every issue and challenge that was thrown at them. They were growing and succeeding as business owners, and the value of their investment was climbing steadily at about 17 percent per year. Another year later, James reduced his time in the office to an average of about one day per week; he still owned 85,000 of the 100,000 outstanding shares of the S corporation.

At this point, the business had grown to almost $3 million in value. The three next-generation owners had paid down a significant amount of their promissory notes, and all three got along very well; a leader emerged from their midst and, to no one's surprise, it was not James's daughter—she wanted to be an owner and a key role player, but not the "captain on the bridge." The three investors ran most of the office and enjoyed the opportunity to think for themselves and figure things out even though the hours were long and the weekends short. James served as a mentor, continuing to check in daily from wherever he was as he thrived in semiretirement. He still was the signatory on the bank accounts, signed the checks, and paid the payroll; in fact, those duties took up most of the time he spent supervising the business operations.

But by now, it had been a couple of years since James had last met with the company's largest clients; he hadn't even met most of the newest clients. He was growing impatient with what amounted to a 20-year succession plan launched too late in his career—15 more years seemed like an eternity. He wanted to retire now, in full, and he needed about $2.5 million at long-term capital gains tax rates to do so. Fortunately, his 85 percent ownership stake came pretty close to solving that problem. Unfortunately, while the investors didn't have $2.5 million, they realized for themselves that they, too, had a choice to make—a hard one, at that.

As James reduced his working hours, a predictable result occurred. The investors realized that while they cumulatively owned only 15 percent of the business, at least in terms of stock, and had paid for just more than half of that, they actually controlled almost 100 percent of the assets—specifically, the client relationships. In other words, the value of the stock that James owned quickly began to take a backseat to the value of the assets that the investors could exert control over. If the ownership team walked across the street and the three of them hung out their own shingle, they'd likely capture most of the business and pay little or nothing for it. They'd all be million-aires in terms of equity value, and have some great paychecks as well with the start of a new business—a rare but enviable opportunity. The alternative was that they could each sign a promissory note for about $850,000, or a combined note from the business for $2.55 million and personally guarantee that debt, and work for the next 10 years to fund James's retirement plan with after-tax dollars before their turn came.

But this particular story has a more pleasant ending. James's succession team did not come out and threaten him or his retirement. Instead, they negotiated from a position of strength, a position that held little resemblance to the 15 percent minority interest they owned and had not even finished paying for. The principle of the 30-hour threshold covered back in Chapter 2, as applied to this fact pattern, is this: Transfer stock at a rate proportionate to the founder's physical control over the assets. If you separate the two issues, the stock could lose some or all of its value over time. This is a basic but important and often overlooked rule in transitioning a professional services practice. James and his succession team had to find another solution, and they did.

The facts were pretty simple. James wanted just over $2.5 million for his majority interest in the business he founded and a small but ongoing role in the business for a reasonable salary. The next-generation advisor/owners wanted to own the business but had no money of their own outside of the business's cash flow, though they did cumulatively own a 15 percent equity stake in a $3 million business. It was time for a transfer of control and ownership. But how to make that happen?

The answer they chose was to utilize a popular attribute of many of today's internal succession plans: accelerating the process by using bank financing to support the transaction. For founding owners who start the process too late or simply find that life, health, or other interests necessitate a more rapid conclusion to their plans, bank financing may provide the answer. This strategy provided James with most of the money he wanted, in cash, thereby reducing his risk, and provided the next-generation advisor/owners a decade of business cash flow and growth from which to pay the debt, leaving capital free to further grow the business, which they were more than excited about.

As a part of the deal's terms, James agreed to remain on board for the next 12 to 18 months on a part-time basis to help with the transition; to be available to sit in on meetings with larger or more difficult clients; and to transition the banking relationships, bookkeeping, and payroll functions over to the new CFO of the company, a possible future owner as well.

The three advisor/owners decided on a more appropriate ownership structure going forward that reflected their risk in the transaction and their anticipated roles, titles, and hours worked over the next 10 years. The rigid structure of their S corporation and its predictable cash flow model helped them create a solid foundation for an enduring business organization that would, with a good plan, outlive each of them as second-generation owners.

This case study is the real thing. Having taken this opportunity to look over the shoulder of one of your peers and learn from his experiences, it is time to solve the problems and to start building that enduring business model and taking control of your future.

CHAPTER 9

Course Corrections

So, you have a succession plan, and you've put it in writing and done the computations. It is going to change. Make that part of the plan. That's part of the fun. That is what owning a business is all about, and that is why independent advisors are such a special group of people.

RETURNING TO THE HARBOR

The first launch of our Lifestyle Succession Plan occurred relatively recently, only about six years ago. Since Tranche 1 in the planning process takes, on average, about five to seven years to complete, we now have our first group of "shipbuilders" coming back in and preparing for Tranche 2. The tales of their journey are fascinating and provide an excellent opportunity to learn from other advisors (G-1, G-2, and G-3) firsthand. This is part of the continuing evolution of the planning process.

About one-third of the businesses reported that the plans had gone more or less as expected and with good results—results that certainly justified the immediate start of Tranche 2. The common struggles seemed to center on finding the right people to support the plan and the business interests. Another third of the businesses reported that while the plan did its job and worked as expected, it took too long and/or they started too late and they needed to accelerate the process substantially. Fairly, about half of those that wanted to accelerate the process were driven not by G-1's preferences, but by the preferences of the succession teams. G-2 and G-3 level owners confidently sought out bank loans or reset the plans to buy out G-1 at a much faster pace—in two or three tranches, not four or five. We found this aspect to be interesting, and somewhat ironic, given G-1's almost universal trepidation over whether G-2/G-3 prospects have what it takes to be an owner. The moral of this story is: Don't wait too long to build your ship and staff it with owners, or you may end up walking the plank.

The last third of the shipbuilders decided that it was not for them and resigned themselves to selling the business or merging when the time came. The common reasons seemed to center on a lack of time and resources to build an enduring business, sometimes starting way too late, or sometimes simply not having the acumen or the energy to do it. As we said many pages ago, set up plan A, the internal ownership strategy, and give it a try. If it doesn't work, there's always plan B, with an average of 50 interested buyers or merger partners ready to step forward at a moment's notice.

This was the first group of business builders that we were able to study and learn from, and, frankly, practice on, so the results are promising even as the systems and procedures continue to evolve rapidly. Taking into account the changes that were made to each group's organizational, entity, and compensation structures, a .666 batting average would get us into the Baseball Hall of Fame, but we really think that the one-third failure rate can and will be improved on by starting earlier, better preparing the industry-wide support systems (coaches, broker-dealers, custodians, insurance companies, regulatory structures), the valuation approach, and the diagnostic tools, and attracting a larger pool of qualified G-2 and G-3 candidates who understand how to select businesses with a future. All these things will come, and many are already in progress.

This is the first generation of independent owners that have had to navigate these seas—the first generation that is retiring with the most valuable of all professional service models in their wake. In the opening chapter, we lamented the fact that only about 5 percent of advisors have ever had a formal valuation to determine their equity value, which implies that 95 percent still value only their cash flow. Maybe the better perspective is that the independent financial services industry has moved out of the shadow of the wirehouse/captive model and in just a generation or two has come to appreciate the differences, the opportunities, and the benefits of being an independent advisor. The next step is to build enduring businesses—5 percent down or in process, 95 percent to go.

EMPOWERING THE NEXT GENERATION

One of the most enjoyable parts of the succession planning process for us is talking to G-2 and G-3 advisors and their spouses about what is typically a first-time ownership opportunity. During these conversations, the usual questions come up: Where does the money come from? What happens if this doesn't work out? Does the profit-based note or our ability to pay it off affect our credit scores? What are the tax implications? But our favorite question is this: How will things be different after we become owners? That's a great question.

Our answer is something like this: On the day after you become an owner, you will likely come in to work at the same time. You'll park in the same space. You'll hang your coat on the same hook, or hanger. You'll sit at the same desk and answer the same phone and do the same things you did the day before you became an owner, and you'll earn the same amount of money. What comes next—what changes and what improves—is up to you and your fellow owner(s).

Over the course of the first year, more things probably remain the same than change. That surprises a lot of first time owners. Restructuring ownership-level compensation has little impact in year one, as the planning process tends to start slowly. Profit-distribution checks will issue once a quarter, but it will take a year or two of growth for that cash flow stream to make an impact. None of that changes the fact that, from the clients' perspective, the business is growing stronger and younger. What's missing is experience. Buying stock and signing a promissory note to pay for it is not enough to transform an employee into an owner, at least beyond the legal sense. It takes something more.

G-1 will have to relinquish some roles and loosen the reins a bit as the former and accomplished dictator (a term we use respectfully); this is no longer a one-person show. One way to do that is to provide G-2 and, in time, G-3, with the appropriate titles, roles, and duties that come with being an owner (COO, CFO, CIO, senior vice president, vice president, etc.), once capabilities have been proven and the titles have been earned. Dare we mention the workload and the worries that are built into this part of the process? But they are part of the process. Share the wealth, share the workload.

As G-1 gradually cuts back on work hours per his or her planned work-week trajectory, G-2 and G-3 level advisors will have to learn to pick up the load, in addition to gradually assuming responsibility for the production as well. Each business will find its own path and pace on these goals and responsibilities. It will take some exploration and experimentation; that's part of the process.

To G-1, we have this message: Give G-2 and, eventually, G-3 level owners the room to learn, and to grow, and to fail. No, they won't do everything like you've done it and they won't do things as well as you've done them, but they will find a way, if you give them your support and guidance and patience. Remember, this is not a competition; the goal is to build an enduring and valuable business with a collaborative team of professionals, and in doing so, they are as new at this as you are. Enjoy the process; don't fight it.

GROWTH IS A SIGN THAT YOUR PLAN IS WORKING

We track growth rates with data gathered from each of the thousands of comprehensive valuations we perform. From this data we know that financial professionals in a one-owner practice (the typical model in this industry) have the highest sustained revenue growth rates when the owner is between ages 45 and 55 at an average compound rate of 13 percent per year. One-owner practices whose owners are between ages 56 and 65 have an average compound growth rate of less than half that rate, about 6 percent, but trending downward, and owners over the age of 65 have negative revenue growth rates of just under −3 percent—these practices are in attrition mode.

The net number of new clients provides an advanced warning system of what is about to happen for each age group of owners. For financial professionals between ages 56 and 65, the net new client rate levels off at around age 58 to 60 and then tracks negative, even though in a good to strong economy the top-line revenue numbers will still track positively and may even look strong, or at least stable. For the group of owners over age 65 in a one-owner practice, both data sets are typically negative.

The leading cause of these declining growth trends is obvious: As advisors get older and achieve many of their personal financial goals, they simply don't invest the same amount of time and energy and money into the business as they once did. The practice is on cruise control, but it is slowly losing speed and momentum. The effort to stay on top of modern technology and each new software release begins to wane. Owners take Friday afternoons off and then the entire day. Three and four-day weekends no longer require an official holiday. As entrepreneurs and independent owners, this is a well-deserved benefit and reward. But as the client age demographics for the remaining client base begin to climb and with too few younger, new clients to balance things out, the practice begins to decline, bleeding off the equity value as the cash continues to diminish gradually.

Succession plans have the ability to reverse these trends and even stop them in their tracks. In the businesses where there are two or more generations of owners (a minimum of 10 to 15 years between each generation is sufficient), and especially those in which an internal ownership track has been established, we're seeing an interesting result. The average age of the ownership team determines which growth rate level the practice or business falls into. For example, a 63-year-old founder who owns 80 percent of an advisory practice set up as an S corporation and a 38-year-old junior partner who owns 20 percent have an average age of just over 50 and tend to have an average compound growth rate in the 10 percent to 15 percent range. As the succession plan is gradually implemented, the client demographics level out over time, the cash flow increases, and the value climbs even as the founder gradually reduces his or her hours worked. G-1 and G-2 advisors often refer to this as the "rejuvenation effect."

While the early data are quite promising, this isn't quite a plug-and-play system. These results require a good plan, built with good, reliable information, and professional equity management. But when equity is managed well and the next generation has access to this opportunity, the results can be amazing.

WHAT TO DO WHEN YOUR PLANS CHANGE

Assume that this is a possibility, even a likelihood, and build an exit ramp into your plan and your documentation.

The whole purpose of a succession plan is to help your business outlive you, so count on this being a long process. As you've learned in previous chapters, while some plans on paper may go out 20 or more years, they are implemented tranche by tranche, with planned opportunities for reassessment and course changes or adjustments. At a minimum, plan for annual valuations to monitor value, annual benchmarks using that valuation data to track operational numbers, and plan adjustments every five years or so. Depending on the size of the business, the number of owners, and the goals, some businesses and firms prefer more frequent maintenance so that the course corrections are more subtle.

While there are many reasons why your plans could change, let's address the more common ones. First is a health issue or a similar concern that causes you (G-1) to want to significantly accelerate your end of the plan. Second is a dissatisfaction with the performance of the business in the hands of your successor team; perhaps they are just not taking on their responsibilities or you're still the largest producer of revenue by a wide margin and you don't see that changing. Third, you decide that what you really want is a lump-sum payout, a large one at that, and you'd like to be done with the whole thing and allow your team to take over and go their own way.

In reverse order, if you want to cash out, see the previous section on bank financing. Bank financing is possible, even likely, if you've set up your plan correctly. You can be substantially cashed out at today's tax rates, and your succession team gets 10 years to pay for the business out of its cash flow and future growth. It can be a win-win, if everyone is ready. The tale of ownership in Chapter 8 also provides an interesting example along these lines.

If the succession team isn't stepping up to your satisfaction and you're unable to resolve that problem with your business partners, then sell the business to the best-qualified third party and be done with it, when the time is right—but don't wait too long. Once you go into attrition mode, value falls fast. To retain the needed level of authority to sell or merge the business, you'll need to have your plan documents prepared with this possibility in mind. Among the tools you'll need are drag-along rights and probably tag-along rights, which are part of the paperwork, at least in the early stages of most succession plans. This is also why you need annual valuations to track the equity number and to make decisions proactively and on a fully informed basis.

Finally, if a serious health issue strikes you or a loved one, there are a couple of ways to address this in terms of your participation in your own succession plan. First, consider this one of the benefits of owning a business with a strong and collaborative team (remember Chapter 5 on continuity planning?). This is a major benefit of having a succession plan and why we encourage you to plan at multiple levels, including the what-if challenges. If your succession team is strong enough and you'd prefer to wrap it up, accelerate the process. Many plan participants call us in the middle of Tranche 1 and roll the plan over into Tranche 2. The process requires some obvious plan adjustments and a new set of paperwork, but to put that in perspective, it usually takes less than one month to make that course correction.

In short, your plans will change one way or another. A good succession plan assumes this fact and provides for frequent and sometimes severe course corrections. Enjoy the ride.

WHAT TO DO WHEN THEIR PLANS CHANGE

This one is a little trickier and harder to plan for. The first thing to consider here is what you always tell your clients about their investments—diversify your risk.

There are several reasons why a succession plan starts by widening the ownership base. The one that is relevant to this discussion is pretty simple: Supporting an enduring business and being part of the succession team as a G-2 or G-3 level owner represents a lifetime commitment, and some younger owners simply won't stay with it for the duration. There could be partnership disputes, health issues, a spouse's relocation or career change, a divorce, a change in vocation, or even a recession. Your stellar G-2 advisor could get a more attractive offer from a larger competitor, or decide to start his or her own business. Stuff happens to everybody, but it seems to happen more frequently and with less warning to those in their 20s or 30s.

This is why you should never tie your future plans, and the value of a business it has taken a lifetime to build, to any one key staff member (and that includes family members) to succeed you—though we often make an exception for a next-generation advisor in his or her 40s or 50s. In addition, having more owners (i.e., widening the ownership base) lowers the cost and risk of the investment to G-2 and G-3 advisor/owners, making the process less demanding and onerous for them.

Second, and it bears repeating, *do not give your stock away.* If you don't place real value on what you've built, neither will your successor or succession team. Have your business formally and authoritatively valued once a year because it is an important and valuable asset, and that is, of course, what you do as a financial professional with any asset you own that is worth six or seven figures and growing. Share those results with your team and *sell the stock*, in small amounts; people tend to value what they work for and have to earn, and they don't easily leave valuable, hard-earned assets behind.

Finally, create an ownership position that matters, something that really makes a difference. We don't mean that your G-2 owners should have their names on parking spaces out front of your building, but we do mean that you need to sell them enough stock that a change in their plans or their lives revolves around this business opportunity and not some other. Plan on each G-2 next-generation prospect owning at least 10 percent in Tranche 1, most through a sale and maybe a little through a granting process if, and only if, they complete the tranche and make that last payment. If G-2 stays through the end of Tranche 1, our thinking and experience indicates that they're committed for the duration.

HANDLING THE CULTURE SHIFT

We worked with a group in Florida several years ago that was owned and run by a husband-and-wife team, both in their early 60s. Rob and Diane had no children in the business, but they did have one key employee, Mark, who was quite capable, though young at age 29. The owners admittedly were starting the succession planning process very late, but after more than 30 years as financial professionals and entrepreneurs they wanted to cut back their work hours substantially and quickly. They were adamant that they did not want to sell and walk away. They felt strongly, after reading and studying and weighing their options, that an internal sale was best for them and their clients.

So they turned to Mark and offered to sell him 49 percent of the business. They would finance the deal, of course, but they wanted Mark to take on the role of president immediately and begin to assume increased responsibility for the operations. Mark agreed, but seized on his opportunity and bargained for the ability to purchase a controlling interest if the business did well over the next 24 months. They set up a series of benchmarks to quantify the hurdles and documented the transaction. Rob and Diane went to half-time status within a year's time, well below the 30-hour threshold. Mark worked long, hard hours and with the winds of a good economy at his back, easily achieved the financial goals.

As the controlling owner, Mark decided to bring in a friend of his to help him, promising an ownership opportunity when it came time to buy out the rest of Rob and Diane's ownership. Together they worked hard, and they began to make the business their own. After every extended vacation, Rob and Diane returned to an office that looked and ran very differently than the one they'd built and, while pleased with the financial progress, watching the change was very hard. They felt their culture had been abandoned, and they felt hurt. Rob and Diane no longer wanted to be involved, so they sold their remaining ownership at fair market value and stepped out of the business for good, but not on great terms.

When advisors sell their practices to a third party, one that is larger and better financed, they understand and expect that their culture will be absorbed by the buyer and replaced. That's part of the deal in most cases. An internal sale is supposed to provide a different result, and it can, if next-generation owners have time to immerse themselves in the business's culture and can appreciate it. As a G-1 level owner, if you go too fast, often a result of starting too late, culture gets traded in like a used car.

If your culture and the identity of your firm are important to you, take steps to preserve those aspects by teaching them to your handpicked succession team. At the same time, don't be afraid of improving on the current state. Work with your partners and make the course corrections gradually, as a team, over a period of decades. To do that, you need to surround yourself with people you trust, and you need to start the process earlier in your career. Make teaching and transition and respect for history a part of your culture, and it will carry your business and your team into the next generation.

Conclusion

Congratulations! If you've read all the preceding pages and made it to this point, you've graduated from practice ownership and you understand how to build something that will be greater than any one person, something that can outlive you and take care of your trusting clients for generations to come. You hold in your hand the keys to your own business.

You've also learned that the process of creating and implementing a succession plan is all about building for the future. It has almost nothing to do with ending your usefulness to your clients or staff—in fact, just the opposite. Succession planning is about growth and collaboration and cooperation and trust; those are the stepping-stones that create a path into the future envisioned by the contributors to this book. But we fully recognize that you're more than a business, and your future is about more than just making money.

In these many pages, we've provided the steps and the strategies and the tools to help you build a valuable business, but ultimately a business is not about these things any more than your home is about its wooden frame and concrete foundation. In the end, it is about you. Your work and what you leave behind are a reflection of you and your values and priorities. Whatever it is you choose to build, picture that day in the future when you do stop, look back, and take inventory of your accomplishments, your successes, and your failures. What is it that will make you most proud? We trust that the steps you take today to better care for your clients, your staff, and your family through the work that you do will be important pieces in your own mosaic.

The independent financial services industry is a special place. In terms of number of advisors and annual revenue growth rates, this model just plain works. One of the reasons the independent sector has grown as fast as it has is through competition, and to be certain, entrepreneurs are great competitors. But there is a key component that is missing, and that is history. As an independent advisor, it is hard to plan successfully for the future when you have little history to look back on and learn from, but that is exactly what you must do. As an independent advisor, you're in charge of what happens next, and you're in charge of creating the history that next-generation advisors will learn from. It is up to you, and us, with help and support from your broker-dealer, custodian, insurance company, and business coach. We have to figure this out together and we have to get started immediately.

Value what you do, literally. You already know what your cash flow is, so take step one and submit to the process of a formal valuation, and put equity to work for you immediately. Share the results of your formal valuation with your spouse, significant other, your business coach, your kids, and your staff; show them your history, and then get busy building an even better future. Equity in the right organizational and entity structure, with a good plan, will lead next-generation talent into your business and, maybe, into your circle of ownership. From there, anything is possible and everything starts to move forward and under your control.

You wanted to own something of your own. You've done that. Now that your future belongs to you and you know what is possible, what will you do with it?

About the Companion Website

This book includes a companion website, which can be found at www.wiley.com/go/successionplan. The companion website contains tools, worksheets, and checklists for the major topics covered in the book.

To access the site, go to www.wiley.com/go/successionplan (password: fptransitions01).

About the Author

David Grau Sr., JD, has spent almost half his life in the financial services industry, as a regulator, as a securities attorney, as a mergers and acquisitions (M&A) specialist, and for the past 16 years at the helm of FP Transitions as its founder and president. FP Transitions pioneered the open marketplace concept of practice transition for the financial services industry beginning in 1999, and now assists independent reps and advisors in all facets of practice valuation, equity management, and succession planning. David is the author of more than 85 nationally published articles, white papers, and manuals, and writes over 1,000 pages of new material per year on these and related topics.

David was named one of the most influential people in the profession in an industry survey of financial advisors by *Financial Planning* magazine and is a nationally recognized expert on succession planning in the financial services industry. He is also one of the nation's leading speakers and instructors on equity management and succession planning issues, practice value and valuation, and long-range strategic exit plans, having delivered over 750 presentations and workshops. He now lives in Portland, Oregon, with his wife Penny, their two sons, three grandchildren, and four rescued dogs.

Index